The Oyster Seekers

The Oyster Seekers

MANDY BRUCE

metro

Published by Metro Publishing Ltd,
3, Bramber Court, 2 Bramber Road,
London W14 9PB England

www.blake.co.uk

First published in paperback in 2006

ISBN 1 84358 136 1

British Library Cataloguing-in-Publication Data:

A catalogue record for this book is available from the British Library.

Design by www.envydesign.co.uk

Printed in Spain by Bookprint SL

1 3 5 7 9 10 8 6 4 2

Papers used by Metro Publishing are natural, recyclable products made from
wood grown in sustainable forests. The manufacturing processes conform to
the environmental regulations of the country of origin.

To all the fishermen of the Thames Estuary, especially Richard Wheeler, Fred Fitt and Ray Gilson.

Acknowledgements

Delia would like to thank everybody who's worked in Wheelers over the last 150 years and those who work there today, especially Angela, Emma, Gavin, Nicky, John, James and Margaret. Also, the Gilson, the West and the Waters families, Brian Hadler, Morgan Davies and Grandad George for encouraging Mark to work hard and fulfil his potential.

Mark wants to add a big 'thank you' to his mum, Anne-Marie, and his dad, Mick, and also Uncles John and Mick. 'I also want to say, "Thanks, Delia, for giving me the opportunity to do what I do best and love most."' Also, a big thank you to Sid Phillis and to my sister Eve.

I would like to thank all my friends in Whitstable, especially Steve and Julia, Karen and Peg. Also, thanks to everyone who contributed such wonderful pictures and drawings, especially Steve Keeler and Christian Furr. Special thanks, too, to ICH and TBS2001 for they know what. Also thanks to John for his faith and friendship, to Michelle for her patience, to Graeme for his talent and thanks Marisa for your enthusiastic and unceasing research! And, as always, thanks Ross.

Finally, Delia and Mark would like to thank their vast and varied army of customers who help make Wheelers the unique place it is today. Customers have been nagging them for years to do a book – this one finally did it!

Mandy Bruce

the oyster seekers

Contents

the oyster seekers

Eternal Father, strong to save,

Whose arm doth bind the restless wave,

Who bidd'st the might ocean deep

Its own appointed limits keep;

O hear us when we cry to thee

For those in peril on the sea.

O Saviour, whose almighty word

The winds and waves submissive heard,

Who walkedst on the foaming deep,

And calm amidst its rage didst sleep:

O hear us when we cry to thee

For those in peril on the sea.

O sacred Spirit, who didst brood

Upon the chaos dark and rude,

Who bad'st its angry tumult cease,

And gavest light and life and peace:

O hear us when we cry to thee

For those in peril on the sea.

O Trinity of love and power,

Our brethren shield in danger's hour;

From rock and tempest, fire and foe,

Protect them whereso'er they go:

And ever let there rise to thee

Glad hymns of praise from land and sea.

W. Whiting, *For Those At Sea*

('The Seafarers' Hymn')

the oyster seekers

Welcome to Wheelers

the oyster seekers

On the East Coast, in the county called 'The Garden of England', lies 'The Pearl of Kent' – the seaside town of Whitstable.

It's easy to miss if you're speeding to the sands and fun of Margate and Ramsgate or inland to the historical glories of Canterbury, but take a left before these places and there, at the top of the hill, you will catch your first glimpse of the sea and the town. Continue on down the hill, past the windmill once owned by the family of famous Victorian actor Henry Irving, and under the railway bridge that, for decades, has carried trains full of holidaymakers travelling south from London. Then, just before the Duke of Cumberland pub, where the road separates – an area once known as The Corner, where dredgermen used to wait for their money from the Oyster Company – there it is: a little pink and blue shop. Welcome to Wheelers. The original Wheelers.

In the front there's a fish bar that hasn't changed for years. You can still buy jellied eels or prawns, cockles and mussels, lobsters and crabs, to eat in or take away. Walk through to the back parlour and there are still only four tables. The old coat stand with its bell for attention still stands by the door, the tablecloths are still covered with glass and you still have to bring your own wine (which involves frantic dashes across the High Street to the off-licence, conveniently situated opposite). Delia Fitt, who has run Wheelers forever, bustles in and out as always, the atmosphere is often chaotic but somehow relaxing at the same

time and, out in the modern back kitchen, young superchef Mark Stubbs and his team create modern fish dishes to make your mouth water. Plaice, haddock, cod, skate – and then, of course, there are the oysters. By cooking and serving local fish and local oysters, Delia and Mark are, between them, carrying on a tradition that goes back for thousands of years. Archaeologists have found numerous old oyster shells in prehistoric sites, not only by the shore but also at inland sites such as the Belgae settlement, which was on the site of Canterbury before Roman times. The Romans loved their Whitstable oysters. They found the British somewhat behind the times, but as the writer Sallust said in about 60BC: 'The poor Britons, there is some good in them after all, they produce an oyster!'

The people of Whitstable, called Witesnestable in the Domesday Book of 1086, have always been sturdy, resilient characters. They've seen it all. They've seen invaders come and go, including the Vikings, the Normans and the Romans; they have always fished and tried to make the most of their most valuable resources: the people and the oysters.

Over the centuries, the oyster beds and dredging rights were 'owned' by a succession of people and organisations. The Church has had possession for much of the time, as have royalty and the aristocracy. In 1790 they were owned by Lord Bolingbroke, but he had to sell them when, true to his name, he went broke. That was when the oystermen got organised and – with the help of a £20,000 mortgage, a fortune in those days – set up The Whitstable Oyster Fishery Company. They restocked the beds and, in 1793, were established legally by a private member's bill in Parliament. It was then that the rules of the Company, which were to last for over a hundred years, were set down.

Working the oyster beds demanded a lot of co-operation between fishermen, therefore everyone had to agree to the rules.

Once a year a 'water court' was held, where decisions about the future fishing and dredging would take place. Men who owned their own boats became Freemen of the Company and paid an annual rent for the right to fish, which was settled by the Company. The eldest son of a Freeman could become a Freeman at the age of 16; other members of the family were granted the same privilege if they had served an apprenticeship of seven years. Each year at the water court, 12 'jurors' were elected to run the Company, an elected bailiff kept an eye on the health of the oyster beds, and there were foremen who controlled the day to day dredging, agreeing with the jury on

At the front of Wheelers is a fish bar that hasn't changed for years.

how many oysters should be the quota for that day's catch. There was to be a closed season from May to August when no dredging was allowed, leaving the oysters alone to 'spat' (spawn) and fatten in peace, but throughout the rest of the year market-boats – known as 'hoys' – were anchored in the bay. Watch boats patrolled night and day to deter poachers. Each oyster smack caught its quota and took the oysters to the hoys, which then sailed up the estuary to the fish market at Billingsgate and London.

The rules that the oystermen made for themselves were strict. You caught your quota and no more. A foreman might search your boat to see if you had hidden any oysters to sell on the side and if you were caught bringing any ashore you were fined 2 pence per oyster – and it didn't go down well at the water court. This rule continued for as long as the Company was in the control of the oystermen but it was always being broken. One oysterman was caught with 70 oysters stuffed down inside his thigh-length boots. In later years, when the men wore oilskins, they found that the deep pockets were ideal for carrying stone jars. They would open a couple of dozen oysters on board and put them in the jars. Then they would go home and put some bacon in a pan on the fire, throw in the oysters at the last minute, cook them in the bacon fat and, with a big chunk of bread, they had made the perfect breakfast to follow a hard night and morning's fishing.

The annual water court, usually held at the end of July before the start of the new season, was a serious occasion when the new jury and officers were elected, but it was also a great excuse for a big party. The streets were hung with bunting and flags, the fishermen dressed in their best white jerseys, and there was feasting on spit-roast beef. The women made a special cake filled with cherries and redcurrants to celebrate the occasion.

The setting up of The Whitstable Oyster Fishery Company marked the beginning of a good century for the town. In the 1770s there were about 22 boats operating off the flats. By the 1790s this had risen to over 70. There were some hard times along the way when, for one reason or another, the oysters didn't spat, but in the 1850s, the beds were restocked, mainly with young oysters – under a year old – from the oyster beds of Normandy. These were shipped home and laid on the local beds to grow for the remainder of their years, taking on all the flavour and subtlety of the waters of Whitstable. This marked the beginning of a boom time. The fleet grew and, in 1862, the Company sent a staggering 60 million oysters to market.

But, apart from the treasure that lay beneath their sea, what really changed the fortunes of the town was the arrival of the 'iron road': the railway. For a hundred years or more, many travellers to

Opposite: **The Wheelers Clan. Front row (*left to right*) Mrs Foreman, Philip, Mary Anne. (Back row, *left to right*) Ellen – Richard's daughter – and Richard Junior – Mary Anne's son.**

the oyster seekers

Canterbury had chosen to travel to Whitstable by ship from London. They then had to disembark on to small boats, an experience which depended for its pleasantness on the swell of the tide. Passengers would then transfer to a coach or cart for the seven-mile journey along the turnpike road to the city of Canterbury. Then, in 1830, the Canterbury and Whitstable Railway Company introduced the first steam-powered passenger and railway service between Canterbury and Whitstable town centre – which rapidly became known as 'the Crab and Winkle line'. Two years later, the railway company cleverly decided to build a harbour at Whitstable, giving shelter to a possible 20 sailing ships. They constructed a dock, extended the railway to the harbour and provided sidings for 80 rail wagons. This worked well for all concerned.

At this time, timber from Prince Edward Island was being brought over by boat, primarily for constructing houses. Once the timber had been unloaded, these boats were sold off cheaply to Whitstable men for them to sail.

Several entrepreneurs made the most of the situation, and the original Captain Wheeler was one of them. Richard Leggy Wheeler was a big man; a dredgerman who, like most of the others, had a strong build and big strong hands – and, allegedly, a twinkle in his eye. By the 1850s he was a Freeman with the Oyster Company, a Master Mariner, regularly dredging for oysters off the Whitstable flats and, in his

boat, *The Cornucopia*, taking advantage of the new railway and making regular trips to Newcastle to pick up a good cargo of coal. He had a keen eye for business. Some time earlier he had married local girl Mary-Anne Foreman, and in 1856 he had the idea of opening a shellfish and oyster bar in the High Street, close to the beach and harbour. It was also close to The Cross – that little area encompassing the Duke of Cumberland pub and The Horsebridge, where many oysters were landed, and where the oystermen often gathered to swap information about the fishing and exchange gossip. It was well placed for the tourist trade too, being close to the beach and with the Rose, now the Royal Naval Reserve pub, just a few doors up. The water court was held here until the Company built the big oyster store on the edge of the beach. The men could bring the oysters ashore here and, in the cellar, was a large oyster store with big tanks of sea water. Above this were the men's assembly rooms, where they could meet and hold the annual court.

With Richard away at sea much of the time, and busy juggling business commitments when he was ashore, it fell to Mary-Anne to run the place. This she did well and, by all accounts, the seafood bar was a handy little profit on the side. This began a tradition which has continued ever since – in the main, Wheelers has been run by women.

Mary-Anne was no shirker and she

knew the sea well. But eventually, after the death of Captain Wheeler, who, it is rumoured, shot himself accidentally when he fell over his game-shooting gun, Mary-Anne was forced to give up the running of the business. She had two sons who might have taken over, but Ernest and Richard junior wanted to be skippers. Richard is said to have died of a heart attack on the beach when he was in his early fifties. Such deaths weren't uncommon. Dredging before the age of automation was even harder than it is now. Many men wore themselves out hand-pulling the dredgers. The dredgers were 5-foot-long, 3-foot-wide bags and could literally weigh a ton as they dredged up boulders, shingle, mud and all sorts of other material along with the precious oysters. Just as maids of the time were called drudges, dredging was also called drudging. Many men also suffered from bronchial problems. Mary-Anne's grand-daughter, Ellen, helped in Wheelers, but when she married, neither her husband, nor their son, Phillip, were interested in fishing.

By the early 1900s the business was still going well but it hadn't been easy. Diseases which killed off the oysters made for a few awful years, and the 'big freezes' around the turn of the century didn't help, but still the original Wheelers kept going. Naturally, the Wheeler family knew most local people and for a short time the oyster bar was run by a man called Philip Browning. Then the running of it was taken over by their friends, the Walsh family – at least by Mrs Walsh. Her son, Bernard, born in an upstairs room at Wheelers, was to play a big part in Wheelers' future.

Originally, the Walsh family came from Waterford, in southern Ireland, where Bernard's grandfather had been a horse dealer, specialising in providing matching pairs for the horse and carriage trade. If the pairs didn't match, a little dye here and there often ensured that they did. When the family moved to Whitstable, Bernard's father joined the oyster trade and Bernard grew up in Whitstable, playing and swimming off the breakers, fishing, poaching oysters and avoiding the watch boats with amazing skill, and generally having a good time. Later he liked to boast that as a teenager he could dig up two thousand lugworms in one tide – still later the boast was that he could open a thousand oysters for lunch with ease.

Bernard grew into a colourful character: tall and powerfully built with bright, blue eyes. Following perhaps in his grandfather's footsteps he was passionate about horses and racing, and game-shooting. He loved the good life, bohemian company, dancing and the theatre. He soon got itchy feet – Whitstable was too small for him. He headed for London and got a job in a West End show – which flopped – and later managed a troupe of dancing girls, who performed in all the casinos along the North Sea coast of Belgium, near Ostend.

But Bernard had also inherited his

grandfather's entrepreneurial spirit and he never forgot Whitstable, his sea – and the oysters. Mother Mrs Walsh continued to run Wheelers, and Bernard soon spotted that oysters had potential. By 1929 he'd moved to London and was looking for premises to open a wholesale business selling fish – and, of course, oysters. He chose an empty shop in Old Compton Street, named it Wheelers, and the famous chain of Wheelers restaurants was born. Within weeks Bernard was selling over four thousand oysters to top London restaurants. Many of the oysters were Royal Natives from Whitstable, and although at seven shillings and sixpence a dozen they weren't top sellers, they were the best. Many people preferred the cheaper, smaller, green-bearded Essex oysters which sold at three and sixpence. But, by now running Old Compton Street as a fish restaurant and oyster bar, Bernard was making a good profit and he was happy. Out of the oyster season he could always retreat back into his Whitstable home shell, where he fished and indulged in his passions of golf, and racing his greyhounds and steeplechasers.

The Second World War brought the Blitz but Wheelers of London stayed open throughout, a lining of corrugated iron inside the windows providing a little cover and a cosy atmosphere, although next to no protection. After the War was over the place enjoyed a new lease of life as it attracted a crowd of bohemians and bon viveurs. It became home of the famous Thursday Club: a group of life-loving, witty, intellectual, like-minded men who loved to meet up, gossip and tell stories. They consumed huge amounts of champagne – and oysters – and enjoyed inventing ridiculous practices such as the extension of the British weekend from Thursday to Tuesday and the adoption of a Champagne-Charlie-For-The-Day. This involved the assembled company singing old music hall songs with such enthusiasm until, as one member put it, 'Wheelers rumbled with the noise'. All the time they were quaffing their oysters and drinking their way through a rehoboam of champagne, a bottle even bigger than a jeroboam, which stood as high as the dining table.

The original Wheelers in Whitstable survived the War too. It stayed open, although the windows were protected by brown cardboard rather than corrugated iron. The bombers often seemed to come perilously close as they tried to bomb the shipyards close to the beach before making their way up the estuary to attack London. The fish and chip shop close by was lost, as was a whole row of terraced houses just a few streets away from Wheelers. After the War, while Bernard was enjoying the bright lights and his new, sophisticated friends, Wheelers, the original little oyster bar we know today, carried on as it always had selling fresh fish, shellfish and, of course, oysters.

Now it was run by Fred Fitt and his family. Fred was a fisherman, although he'd come to fishing in a roundabout way. He'd run away with the gypsies when he was just 11, then tried his hand at jobs in London in pubs and restaurants before returning to Whitstable to work the boats. And while Fred fished, his wife ran Wheelers. Martha, a glorious redhead, showed herself more than capable of running the shop, making the customers feel at home in the back parlour with good shellfish lunches and a lot of smiles. As the sophisticates enjoyed Bernard's hospitality and celebrated the end of the War with oysters and champagne in Old Compton Street, the natives down in Kent were doing the same, sometimes with whelks, sometimes with winkles and prawns, and oysters, of course, usually washed down with brown ale or stout.

After the War the tourists began to come back on the 'iron road'. The beaches were cleared of the barbed wire that had been placed there to prevent invasion although everyone knew that the wire wouldn't have kept the invading Germans off for very long. There were still several unexploded bombs lying around the town, which were gradually cleared up – one was discovered during building work for a new house in the 1970s. But the sun shone, the boarding houses and B&Bs along the front re-opened, the sea was fresh to swim in and fish was caught again. What was more, the oysters appeared to have survived it all, although reviving the industry was hardly plain sailing – or dredging! The end of the War brought great celebrations but, in many ways, it was

not the end but the beginning of a very hard time for the oystermen. The winter of 1947 was freezing and cruel – and if there is one thing oysters cannot stand it is icy cold. Then came the floods of 1953, when almost half the town was submerged by furious tides. Pictures survive of residents being carried off the roofs of their houses by helpers in rowing boats. Many oyster beds were wiped out and the final disaster came in early 1963. Once again it was exceptionally cold with icy winds and chilling waters. These were desperate times for the oyster industry.

The original Wheelers kept going – there were always the eels, the cockles, the mussels, the winkles and whelks – and Martha was always there with a friendly welcome. Oysters were few.

Fred Fitt continued to fish, until a lorry, pulling out of a slip road close to the harbour, hit his car and injured him to such an extent that he was never able to go aboard a boat again. A heavy smoker, he died of emphysema when he was in his sixties. Martha died two years later. Their daughter Delia had been working in Wheelers when she wasn't at school or college but she had no intention of going into the fish trade. She had big plans. But now, with Martha gone, it was up to her to keep Wheelers going. She took over, alone to start with, and then with the help of her cousins.

The oyster trade picked up over the years but it was a slow process. Then in the

1980s the Seasalter and Shellfish Company, a direct descendant of the old Seasalter and Ham Company, was back farming oysters. Their attempts to farm Natives were unsuccessful but the Rockies were farmed first in hatcheries for three months, and then returned to just off the coast for the next two years.

By the 1990s, Whitstable oysters were making a big comeback, and now Whitstable once again lives up to the name given to the town by a periodical in the 1790s: Oysteropolis. You can eat oysters all year round and, thanks to an EU directive, only oysters from Whitstable can now be called Whitstable Oysters.

Whitstable and the oyster trade has survived, and the town has been enjoying a revival. It remains a funny old place of pretty weatherboard cottages and secret alleys with eccentric names, like Squeeze Gut Alley, which links the rows of little Victorian houses. The High Street hasn't changed much, and neither has the beach, which is mostly shingle, proving painful to lie on until you wriggle yourself into a comfortable position while you kick difficult mussel shells into touch. The tide goes out for what seems like miles to reveal the mud where all sorts of sea creatures lurk. When you wander out on to the flats, the mud squishes through your toes and you have to watch you don't sink several feet into the holes dug by people who still come out to dig for lugworms when the tide is low. But put on your wellies and walk at low tide, especially in the early morning or evening, and the light and the space silence you. Look out to sea. To your left are the marshes of Seasalter, once a favourite haunt of smugglers. To your right, beyond the harbour, there are the slopes of Tankerton, where genteel folk used to sit, drink tea and contemplate the horizon from the balcony of the elegant Marine Hotel. Between the Marine Hotel and the harbour, there's The Street, a strange finger of shingle which stretches a mile out to sea at low tide.

The people of Whitstable are an eclectic mix. There are the true natives, born and bred, who never left, and the true natives who left but came back. There are the younger natives who long to leave but usually come back at some point. The town supports some light industry, plenty of retail and service work, but hardly an abundance of good money-making jobs. Many feel they are being priced out of the housing market by the weekenders, so they leave – but many come back.

Then there are the DFLs, as they're called locally (the Down-From-Londons). The latest batch adore the place. Many try to spend their summers here – some never go back. Some like to think they 'discovered' the place – it's their secret –

which the natives, grateful for the business they've brought with them, don't mind – as long as they don't try to turn the place into too much of an Islington-on-Sea. In fact, DFLs have been coming down from London for the summer for hundreds of years. The beach these days can get busy on warm, summer days but not as crowded as when mobile beach bathing huts were introduced in the 1700s. Old photographs from the 1800s show the beach packed with holidaymakers, the ladies sitting in their highly buttoned, full-skirted dresses beneath the shade of their parasols, their menfolk sitting beside them in suits, pressed shirts and ties.

Over the years, the town has always attracted entrepreneurs and it owes much of its recent revival to them. Like everyone else they're welcomed – as long as they don't get too greedy and try to 'take over'. Many entrepreneurs find success, stay and become locals themselves.

There are older retired people and younger students from nearby Kent University at Canterbury. They are passing through but most can't resist coming back at some time.

And there are the students who arrived in the Seventies, got stuck in a time warp – and never went back.

There are dozens of artists and musicians, craftsmen and sculptors. One look at the spectacular sunsets, when the sky turns from electric yellow to orange to red to awesome pink, and the light

reflects on the thin film of water of the mud flats, making the sea and sky one big, extraordinary, multi-coloured light show, and most painters become passionate and grab their brushes. Turner was one such artist – he painted sunsets here.

You also get an awful lot of Weather at the seaside. Living by the sea is inevitably a humbling experience. You can contact the other side of the globe via the net; you can become a space tourist if you are rich enough; you can witness wars as they happen on TV; but if that wind wants to blow, it will. And if that tide wants to come in, it will.

Townies who visit the seaside only on occasion – preferably when The Weather Is Good – are often confused by the language used by the seaside natives of East Kent. Briefly: 'It's nice and fresh today' means it's extremely windy so don't put up your umbrella. 'It's a bit breezy today' means that it's blowing a gale so don't walk on the beach, unless you're prepared to be blown over. 'Oh dear, seems to be blowing up a bit' means you can expect hurricane force winds, so go home, have a nice winkle tea or a prawn sandwich, batten down the hatches and watch the tiles fly off the roof.

People who live and work by or on the sea look at the sky more than others. Fishermen – indeed anyone who has a boat – are acutely wind and weather conscious. There is a standing joke among fishermen, especially the whelkers, who have no more appetite for going out in howling gales and freezing cold than anyone else: hold a lighted candle out of the window. If the flame is blown out, it's obviously too windy to go out. If the flame doesn't go out, then there's no wind so there's no point in going out.

There are many old seaman rhymes about the weather and on the whole they make good sense. Everyone knows the 'red sky at night, shepherds' delight ...' The seaman's equivalent is:

The evening red and morning grey,
Are sure signs of a fine day,
But the evening grey and morning red,
Make the sailor shake his head.

Seasalts know that the tides are likely to be higher – and the weather more volatile – around the times of the full or new moon, and folklore has it that you can forecast rain with the help of a length of seaweed. The idea is that you hang up a big, long bit of seaweed and if it becomes damp then rain is imminent. Unfortunately this isn't always reliable.

Or, following the advice of expert naturalist and dedicated wrecker Tony Soper, in his wonderful book *The Shell Book of Beachcombing*, you can have a go at making your own beach barometer. It may not work, but it's good fun to try.

First, he says, you need to go to the off-licence and buy a bottle of Chianti (you need the bottle with the straw case as these ones are the correct shape). Then you have

to empty the bottle, i.e. consume its contents, rendering you incapable of even saying 'barometer'. Next, having torn off the straw, clean and dry the bottle. Take a big jar and fill it with water. Put the upside-down Chianti bottle into the jar of water. Pour out the excess water so you're left with a jar and an inverted tight-fitting bottle with water that comes up the neck of the bottle, where the cork used to be. And there you have it: your own barometer, which will show changes in atmospheric pressure by the rising and falling of the water level inside the wine bottle.

It will take a few days to settle down, and you must keep it away from direct sunlight and at room temperature. Thereafter, the higher the water rises in the neck of the bottle, the better the weather will be. If the top of the bottle gets misty, then expect light rain. If the top of the bottle gets full of condensation then you're in for heavy rain. If the water at the bottom of the bottle is 'blown out' then, as the natives say, it's definitely 'blowing up a bit'. So expect a hurricane.

And then there are the fishermen. The magnificent sight of the bay, full of red-sailed oyster smacks, full sail in the wind, is no more. The local fleet is small; but at least there is a fleet. Fishing is still a hard business – there's nothing twee about

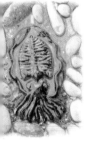

fishing. Despite automation, dredging and catching is still a hard job, especially in winter. Fishing is no get-rich-quick-and-easily business. But, despite that, and despite the mountain of regulations, there are still men who can't imagine any other life. Fish are still caught and oysters are still brought ashore. The old Oyster Stores are still there, although the stores themselves have become a restaurant and the rooms upstairs – where the Water Court used to be – until recently held the town's cinema.

The town has changed, but Whitstable adapts. As they say here, 'Time in Whitstable doesn't march on, it just goes around and around.' In many ways it's like any number of other little seaside towns – yet it's like no other. Of course, some people hate the place. (Somerset Maugham, who grew up here, christened it Blackstable in his book *Cakes and Ale*.) All that mud, no sand, few amusements. But most people who come and go come back. 'I wasn't supposed to be going into the Wheelers business,' says Delia, nonchalantly opening a dozen oysters. 'I mean, I didn't choose the job – it sort of chose me. But I don't regret it. I wouldn't want to be anywhere else. It's like an octopus this place – it always pulls you back in.'

Welcome to Wheelers. Come in.

Cook's
Notes

Take a piece of lovely, fresh, fish – perhaps some plaice or a dab or two – fry or grill for a few minutes with butter, add a squirt of lemon and maybe a twist of black pepper, and serve with some good, crusty bread plus a glass of dry, crisp, white wine – the perfect lunch. Or maybe buy some fresh winkles and a little watercress, slice some brown bread thinly and butter lightly and refresh the watercress in cold water. Serve with some toothpicks to get the little creatures out, a small bowl of malt vinegar on the side for dipping and, of course, cups of nice strong tea. Then again, you may only need some prawns that have been thrown on the barbecue, with a little freshly made garlic mayonnaise, or some sardines, with big wedges of lemon and generous chunks of wholemeal bread.

Fish – simple and plain – is often the best. But if you love fish, and want to have some creative fun with it, here are some of the most popular dishes served in the restaurant today. Some of the ingredients lists may look alarmingly long but most of them are stalwarts of the fish lover's larder and, if you're going to be cooking fish on a regular basis, you'd be wise to stock up on a few essentials.

- Buy a **good virgin olive oil**, some **malt vinegar** and perhaps some **balsamic** (the taste of balsamic vinegar in dressing adds a piquancy that goes wonderfully well in salads accompanying fish). A good supply of **lemons** is almost essential, plus **fresh herbs** – if you can grow your own all the better, especially parsley, chervil and chives.

- **Cayenne** and/or **Tabasco** is always useful, plus **fresh garlic** and **good butter**. Use **sea salt** and **black and white pepper**. Stock up on all these and you're never far away from a good meal. All you need is the loaves, the fishes and, perhaps, some fresh salad leaves. If you want to cook fish dishes, many of the sauces can be made in advance. **Stocks can be frozen** and special extras – like chilli vinegar – will keep for weeks in the bottle.

- Unless you're making something like your own fish stock or soup – which can take time but is well worth the effort

the oyster seekers

buying and keeping fish

When you're buying fish you need to look them straight in the eye. Look for fish with bright eyes – not sunken, dull eyes. If you feel the flesh it should feel firm and moist but shouldn't be slimy. You're buying wet fish but it should feel almost dry and, most importantly, it shouldn't smell unpleasantly fishy, but fresh with a hint of the sea. The gills should be a vibrant red, not dull.

Ideally you should try to buy and cook your fish the same day but that isn't always possible, so you need to store it carefully. Mark is fastidious, even pernickety, about keeping the fish in Wheelers as fresh as possible. The first rule is to prepare your fish – gut it and fillet it, if necessary, as soon as you get it home. Then wash it and pat dry with kitchen paper. Cut into portions if necessary and wrap each one in clingfilm then put on a tray. In the restaurant the fridge trays have holes in them to allow any moisture to drip through to a tray underneath – it's the moisture that causes problems. If you don't have such a tray, cover an ordinary baking tray tightly with foil then prick some holes in it and rest the fish on that. In the restaurant Mark rewraps his fish twice a day. Once

unwrapped for cooking the fish should never smell nasty and fishy – if it does, throw it away. It should always smell freshly of the sea. As a general rule you shouldn't keep fresh fish in the fridge for longer than 48 hours even if wrapped.

But if you're visiting the seaside, or a good harbour shop like Gilson's at Whitstable harbour, you might want to take some fresh fish home with you. In that case, keep it as cold as possible while you're travelling. When home, prepare, gut, fillet and portion it as necessary, wash and dry it and then put it in the freezer. It should come out tasting almost as good as the day you bought it.

Be careful about storing shellfish; always eat them on the day you buy if possible. You might want to freeze fish like prawns but always check with your fishmonger or harbour shop that they haven't been frozen before. Or buy ready-frozen prawns and put them straight in the freezer.

It is possible to freeze a whole crab or lobster, and some customers have been known to buy a freshly-cooked crab and just put it in the freezer whole. They report success, but we don't recommend it as the shell often goes extremely brittle. Better to prepare your fresh crab or lobster first, then freeze it.

Mark doesn't recommend freezing, fresh is best if possible.

Our recipes are here to sample. Don't be afraid to experiment. Some combinations have raised a few eyebrows when they've first been put on the menu but, after they've discovered how well different flavours go together, the customers keep coming back for more.

Try, taste as you go along, but most of all … enjoy.

and can be frozen – fish cooking is fast. You should be able to cook a fantastic meal at the stove in 20 minutues. Most of the cooking is done on the hob, so you will need **quite a few saucepans**. An ordinary **food processor** is invaluable for soups, sauces and vegetables. Some of the dishes here are finished off in the oven so you need **a couple of good baking pans**. A **sturdy sieve** is also a good idea.

- The secret of a good fish meal is **fresh fish** – the fish has the starring role. The supporting cast can be prepared in advance; clean and chop your vegetables, prepare or defrost the sauces, make the mash or purée the vegetables ahead of cooking. Then you literally cook, combine, arrange and serve. Wheelers fish is always cooked to order.

conversion tables

The recipes in this book state amounts in metric rather than imperial measurements. The following table gives the exact conversion from pounds and ounces to grams. One ounce equals 28.35 grams, but most common-sense cooks use 25g as a guideline to slightly under 1oz. One kg equals 2.2lbs.

WEIGHTS		OVEN TEMPERATURES		
oz	g	ºC	ºF	Gas Mark
1	28.35	111	225	¼
2	56.7	130	250	½
4	113.4	140	275	1
8	226.8	150	300	2
12	340.2	170	325	3
16	453.6	180	350	4
		190	375	5
LIQUIDS		200	400	6
1 pint = 568ml		220	425	7
1 litre = 1.76 pints		230	450	8

CHAPTER 1

Oysters

It's rarely love at first sight. To anyone who has never tried one, the opened oyster, with its viscous appearance and sometimes slightly greenish tinge, is anything but appetising. But shut your eyes, eat and there's the taste; it's the essence of the sea in a seashell. The wind, the waves, the ozone, the whole lot is there in a mouthful. Of all the riches of the sea, of all the fish and shellfish, for once it's the fish that catches the man; and once you're hooked, you're hooked.

Oysters are unique in that they are one of the few pleasures in life that give you a terrific 'up', yet they contain a lot of goodness and next to no calories. And they don't cost the earth. Whether or not they're addictive is debatable. Some people cannot stop eating them. As the poet Sir Humphrey Gilbert wrote in the 1500s, of a friend: 'He had often eaten oysters, but had never had enough.'

Delia remembers, when she was a child and her father was a fisherman, watching a man eating 188. 'It took him half an hour. He was an officer in some regiment somewhere and he bet another officer he could eat 200 oysters at one sitting. He didn't quite make it and I don't think he exactly savoured them.'

An oyster should be savoured. To swallow it straight down and get that lovely oomph in one go – or to chew and delay the experience? Now that is a question. The smallest Whitstable 'Natives' – Number Fours – are called 'buttons' and, says Delia, 'I would say that the meat inside a button is like a well-fleshed walnut. And that's what an oyster should be – just a delicious mouthful.

'I always think just to swallow is a bit of a waste. I would say that you crush the oyster in your mouth as if it were a strawberry. You don't chew a strawberry; you crush it in your mouth and get all that flavour of early, sweet summer. It's the same with an oyster; you crush it in your mouth, you squash it and then you swallow, and get all that taste that is pure sea.'

Whitstable oysters are justifiably famous and, arguably, the Natives are the best oysters in the world, although people in Colchester and certain areas of Scotland and Ireland may disagree. Not to mention the east coast of America, 'where,' says Delia, with horror, 'they batter them and serve them with horseradish or *tomato ketchup* – can you imagine?'

The Whitstable Natives are still harvested wild on the oyster flats which stretch out for an area of a mile or so from the Isle of Sheppey to Reculver: the Whitstable flats. The oysters themselves are also called flats because the tops of their shells are flat. The oysters love that mud, and the water in the Thames estuary isn't too salty for them. Other areas cultivate flat oysters, but only

the Whitstable Natives have a little 'thumb' on the side of their shells.

They have been harvested here for many hundreds of years. The Romans used to take Whitstable and Colchester oysters back to Rome, towing them in big baskets behind the galleys; a sensible idea – oysters do like living water, as stagnant water kills them and renders them inedible.

Oysters are regal molluscs. Henry VIII, a true hedonist, consumed hundreds. His daughter, Elizabeth I, apparently loved them and royalty and aristocracy never gave up the habit. Only recently two elderly ladies came into the shop asking for two 'Nines' – that's nine Native oysters each.

'I couldn't help but say: "Oh very Queen Mary,"' says Delia, 'because Queen Mary, in the 1920s and 30s, used to have nine oysters for luncheon every day – no more, no less. Hence the expression.'

Yet before that, in the 1800s, Dickens' time, they were very much the food of the poor. Fisherwomen used to sell oysters – many from Whitstable – from baskets on street corners. The poor used them as food – the rich as delicacies to cleanse the palate before they tucked into the next five courses.

The proper name for Whitstable oysters is *oyster edulis* and you won't eat one younger than four and a half years old in Wheelers, where they sell Natives aged

Whitstable Natives and Rockies.

the oyster seekers

between four and a half and six years old. The old adage of eating oysters only when there is an 'r' in the month still applies to the Whitstable Natives – although these days you can eat them all year round thanks to the development of the Whitstable Rocky oyster or 'gigas'.

True, wild Natives are harvested in the winter months and are available from September to April. If you were to eat a Native in the summer it probably wouldn't do you any harm but it wouldn't be such a pleasant experience. The summer months are when the oyster spawns – 'spats' – in the frilly bits, called the mantle. First of all, the oysters go creamy, like condensed milk, then they start to grow black and unpleasant until the spawn – or spat as it's known at a later stage – are projected by the oyster into the sea to make their own way in life. Each oyster can produce spawn – which looks something like little bits of grit – for over a million oysters, but rarely more than 10 per cent will survive their early days in the sea.

Once they've got to the spawning stage the poor oyster is tired, thin and poor, 'and about as tasteless as a piece of tissue paper,' says Delia. 'So you don't eat them then because they don't taste good and you'd be depriving the world of another generation of Natives.'

When it comes to reproducing, the oyster is an extraordinary creature. The oyster doesn't have to go to all the trouble of finding another oyster mate; by regularly changing sex throughout the year, it manages the entire procedure alone. It matures as a male, changes slowly into a female and continues to alternate sex every year.

When the oyster spats varies from year to year. If the water isn't warm one summer they may spat later; if the water warms early they may spat early. Either way, the winter months, when the oyster has had a chance to fatten up, is the best time to eat them. Even so, despite modern technology, the oyster harvest in any year is unpredictable.

'They are very precious creatures in more ways than one – financially, because you have to wait so long before harvesting them, and in their very lifestyle,' says Delia. 'Like most aristocrats they are fussy. They can catch anything that's going around in the water and then they go into a kind of hysteria, and refuse to spat. They are very sensitive to water temperature and pollution. They are delicate and difficult. They don't like the water too warm or too cold. They don't like it too salty or not salty enough. They like their mud just so.

'Oysters from different areas are different in taste and texture depending on the differences in the water and temperature. But when Whitstable Natives are good, when the conditions have been right, they are the best. They are beautiful, and they are clearer and cleaner-tasting than most oysters.'

True Natives are graded in size from Number Ones to Number Fours – Ones being the biggest and oldest. If you look carefully at their shells you should be able to

HOW TO OPEN AN OYSTER

Opening an oyster, or trying to, when you haven't done it before can be an exasperating and blood-pressure-heightening experience. Experts like Delia make the process look easy, but many an amateur, just longing for that morsel within, have been driven to desperate measures in frustration: they attack them with kitchen knives, hammers and chisels, they throw them against the wall or onto the floor and then jump on them. Rule one is to keep calm.

Ideally, you need an oyster knife which is slightly pointed with a heavy blade and a tough handle. Delia gets her from Sheffield and uses a different knife for Rockies and Natives. The Natives knife is slightly thinner but doesn't have as much leverage so you need to wiggle it more. Every country and every oyster community has a slightly different-shaped oyster knife according to the kind of oysters they farm. If you haven't got a proper oyster knife, use one of those old-fashioned pointed tin openers, the ones that you had to personally pull around the edge of the tin, not the ones you turn.

First, put a folded cloth or a wedge of paper on the surface you're using. This will prevent it slipping and also protect the surface. Oyster shells scratch everything.

Hold the oyster with the slightly pointed, 'hinged' end towards you. Use a cloth, keeping the cloth between your hand and the oyster, as the shell can cut you.

The hard bit is getting the knife into the hinge. Once the knife is in, give it a little twist. (If using the tin opener, once you've got in you can use a vegetable knife). Slide the knife along the inside, from the top of the oyster

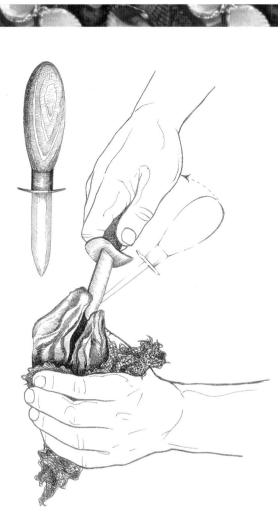

shell to the bottom. This will sever the muscle (the living part of the oyster which holds the whole thing together). Cutting through the muscle opens the oyster. Pull back on the hinge and discard the top half of the shell.

Use your knife to just cut under the oyster and flip it over quickly in the shell, keeping as much of the juice as possible. Then ... eat!

see their age, as they grow 'rings' rather like trees. Each 'ring' is more or less a year.

The Whitstable Natives grow wild, but rockies are now farmed in Whitstable waters by the Seasalter Shellfish Company. The oysters are bred in a succession of filtered

seawater tanks before being packed in mesh bags and laid on trestles in the sea. This allows them to be in their natural element, with plenty of food in the sea and freely circulating water. The gigas are smaller than the Native, the shell deeper,

the oyster seekers

they can be eaten younger and, because they don't take so long to come to edible proportions – three years rather than four and a half – they are considerably cheaper.

Many people are still nervous about eating oysters, associating them with terrifying tales of oyster poisoning, and it's true that the oyster is a filter feeder. But these days the oysters you buy in Britain are purified in running water for at least 36 hours, getting rid of any of what Delia calls 'nasties'. The basic rules of molluscs apply to the oyster as much as they do to the mussel:

NEVER OPEN OYSTERS IN ADVANCE – at Wheelers they are always opened as they are ordered. The oyster shell should always be tightly closed when you buy it – if the shell is open it should be discarded. 'In France you will see oysters open and on display, but I would never eat an oyster like that,' says Delia. 'Ideally you want them opened at the table or at least as they are ordered. Ours are always opened on demand and taken straight to table. Between half an hour and an hour is the maximum you can keep them open, and if it's summer I'd say no more than half an hour. Apart from anything else, they lose their juice, which is part of the pleasure. I think they become a bit like wilted lettuce leaves – and who likes wilted lettuce leaves?

'Many people want to serve oysters at a dinner party and if they live locally we ask them to come half- to three-quarters of an hour before they're to go to table and we will open them and put them on a plate and finish them with lemon wedges or whatever.

'Of course some people buy them to open themselves. We have one customer who has a stream running through his basement and the oysters love that – it's cool and damp – and he puts them deep shell-side down, not in the stream but near, and covers them with a nice, damp cloth. That's what they like – they don't much like the fridge – too cold. Intense cold will kill an oyster as fast as hot intense sun. You really don't want to serve a dead oyster – unless, of course, you've got a very good enemy.'

HOW DO YOU EAT THEM? There are a hundred ways, and Mark and Delia include here some of the best ways of using the gigas in your cooking. But most oyster lovers agree that eating your Whitstable Native straight is best. Some people like a dash of Tabasco, some a tiny sprinkle of cayenne. Many new restaurants think they discovered shallot vinegar, but, in fact, the Edwardians and Victorians were there way before them and the Romans always went for a little lemon juice. You'll need some thinly sliced, lightly buttered brown bread, or not, as the case may be, and perhaps champagne, or a cool glass of Chablis, or a Black Velvet, or, as many gentlemen have done before you, sit there and enjoy a dozen and a pint of Guinness.

Oysters Au Naturel

ingredients

Serves 2 or 4

24 Whitstable Natives or
 Rocky oysters
8 slices of good brown bread,
 thinly sliced and buttered
1 bag of crushed ice
1 lemon, cut into wedges
Tabasco, cayenne or paprika
seaweed
shallot vinegar
 (see recipe page 192)

Simply place the crushed ice on to one central plate or individual plates and scatter a little seaweed over the ice. For decoration, you could use some samphire, which is delicious and edible, or else a bladderwrack, found on beaches, well-washed. Open the oysters (see diagram, page 25), and present them, in their shells, on the ice with the lemon wedges. Serve immediately with the Tabasco, cayenne, paprika or shallot vinegar on the side. This is very much a matter of personal choice. We tend to think that Tabasco is too overpowering for the oyster but many people like that extra kick. Only the bread and butter and the lemon wedges are real musts and, even then, some oyster lovers might argue about the lemon. Enjoy.

Whitstable Rocky Oysters with a Champagne and Lemon Granita

ingredients

Serves 2 or 4

24 Whitstable Rocky oysters
150g granulated white sugar
400ml cold water
750ml champagne
zest of one lemon

Put the sugar and water in a pan along with the lemon zest. Boil for 3 minutes. Add the champagne, bring back to the boil and simmer for 2 minutes. Put the mixture into a metal tray, allow to cool, then when cold put into the freezer. Take a fork to the granita mixture every half an hour and churn it about a bit until it sets and delicate champagne ice crystals have formed. Open the oysters and put a teaspoon of granita on each before serving. Eat immediately.

Angels on Horseback with Watercress Salad

ingredients

Serves 4

12 medium Whitstable
    Rocky oysters
6 to 8 rashers of streaky,
    unsmoked bacon, very thinly
    sliced
2 slices of good white bread
a knob of butter
a few drops of lemon juice
a pinch of cayenne pepper
2 bunches of fresh watercress
1 tbsp balsamic vinegar
2 tbsp good olive oil
12 cocktail sticks

Pick over the watercress and take out the thick stalks and any bits you don't like the look of. Wash very thoroughly and then place in the fridge. Put the vinegar in a bowl with salt and pepper to taste, whisk together and slowly add the olive oil to make a nice, rich dressing.

Open the oysters, saving as much juice as you can in the process. Put the oysters to one side and then pass the juice through a sieve into a pan. Bring the juice to the boil immediately and drop the oysters in for, literally, about 10 seconds. Remove the oysters and put to one side to cool, then wrap each one in half a rasher of bacon. Secure with a cocktail stick and place them side by side in a baking tray.

Grill the bread on both sides until golden and then remove the crusts. Butter and cut in half on the diagonal. Grill the oysters in bacon until they're crispy and golden on all sides. When they're cooked, dress your plates. Toss the watercress in the dressing – not too much – and put some on each plate. Add the toast, then top the toast with the hot oysters – three to each triangle – add a squeeze of lemon juice and a little cayenne.

Angels on Horseback with Soda Bread Served with Baby Spinach and Pine Nut Salad

ingredients

Serves 4

4 tsp vinaigrette

12 Whitstable Rocky oysters

12 slices of streaky bacon, thinly sliced

4 slices of soda bread

50g softened, unsalted butter

1 tsp chopped parsley

½ tsp anchovy essence

1 tsp chopped chervil

a pinch of cayenne

4 lemon wedges

150g baby spinach

60g toasted pine nuts

12 cocktail sticks, soaked in water

Mix the softened butter with the anchovy essence, parsley, cayenne and chervil. Toast the pine kernels until they're light and golden and allow to cool. Open the oysters, put them on some clean kitchen paper to dry slightly, then roll them up in the bacon and secure with a cocktail stick.

Toast the bread and lightly spread with the softened anchovy butter. Preheat the grill, then grill the oysters until the bacon is only just beginning to crisp – don't overcook them. Add the pine kernels to the spinach and dress with the vinaigrette.

To serve, place the salad at the top of the plate, the anchovy toast at the bottom and the hot oysters on top of both. Serve with the lemon wedges.

Grilled Oysters with Parma Ham, Rocket and Parmesan

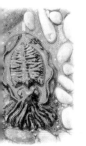

ingredients

Serves 4

24 Whitstable Rocky oysters
(keep the bottom, deeper shells,
discard the top shells)
4 thin slices of Parma ham
squeeze of lemon
1 large shallot
125g rocket
100g fresh Parmesan
good olive oil

Dice the Parma ham into small pieces. Finely dice the shallot. Carefully cut the rocket into small pieces. Open the oysters, reserving the juice and then grate the Parmesan. Sweat the shallot in a little oil for 2 or 3 minutes – don't let it brown – and add the Parma ham. Cook for another couple of minutes. Then add the oyster juice and reduce down to virtually nothing before adding the rocket. Cook briefly until the rocket has just wilted.

Place a little of this mixture in the bottom of the oyster shell, place an oyster on top, add a little bit more of the mixture, sprinkle with a little fresh Parmesan and place under a hot grill for a couple of minutes until the cheese starts to bubble. Add a squeeze of lemon juice and serve immediately.

Grilled Oysters Rockefeller

ingredients

Serves 4

12 large Whitstable Rocky oysters
225g sea salt
1 clove garlic, finely chopped
225g washed fresh spinach
1 dessertspoon chopped parsley
1 pinch cayenne and a squeeze
  of lemon
1 tbsp fine breadcrumbs
1 small shallot, finely diced
1 tbsp double cream
2 tbsp Pernod
olive oil
salt
20g grated fresh Parmesan

Place a little olive oil in a medium to hot pan, add the shallots and garlic and cook for about 2 or 3 minutes. Keep an eye on it and ensure that the mixture does not brown. Add the Pernod and carry on cooking until it has reduced to virtually nothing. Turn down the heat. Add the spinach and allow it to wilt – this won't take long – and add salt and cayenne. Put this mixture into a food processor and blend until smooth. Then add the lemon juice, cream and breadcrumbs. Check. Taste. Season if necessary.

Open the oysters, turn and leave them in their shells. Evenly spread the sea salt over a baking tray to create a bed for the oysters to sit in. Use sea salt if you can because it prevents the oysters from moving around or tilting over. Place the oysters, in their half shells, on the salt. Put a little bit of the spinach mixture over each oyster, sprinkle with the Parmesan and bake in the oven for about 5 minutes. Serve immediately, sprinkled with the chopped parsley.

Whitstable Oysters Coated in Guinness Batter

ingredients

Serves 4

24 Whitstable Rocky oysters
1 x 200ml can of Guinness
4 tbsp cornflour
2 tbsp plain flour
salt
vegetable oil

Make the batter by mixing the cornflour, flour and salt and then slowly adding the Guinness, whisking or beating all the time. Open the oysters and lightly pat dry on kitchen paper. Dry the oyster shells well, so that when you put the battered oysters back in them they will stay nice and crisp. Dip the oysters into the batter mix, then into the oil and fry quickly for no more than 2 minutes. By this time they should be golden and crispy. Serve a battered oyster in each shell.

Large Whitstable Natives Served on a Bed of Warmed Puy Lentils and Coppa Colla

We usually don't recommend cooking with Whitstable Natives at all but this recipe is the exception. If the oysters are really big, this works wonderfully well.

ingredients

Serves 4 as a starter

2 tbsp finely diced carrot,
    shallot and leek
12 large Whitstable Natives
100g puy lentils
1 onion
1 carrot
12 very thin slices of coppa colla
    (cured pork)
few sprigs of fresh rosemary
    and thyme
bay leaf
butter

Soak the puy lentils overnight in cold water. When you're ready to cook the next day, drain the lentils and put into a pan with more cold water, the onion, carrot and herbs. Bring to the boil and simmer for about 15-20 minutes, by which time the lentils should be just tender. Drain, reserving the liquid, place on a tray and allow to cool. When cold, return to the cooking liquor.

Put the butter into a pan, add the finely diced vegetables, and allow to sweat for 2 or 3 minutes without browning. Open the oysters, saving the liquor. Add the lentils and the oyster liquor to the finely diced vegetables in the pan. Season to taste. Remove the oysters from the shells. Put a little of the hot lentil mixture into each half shell, top each with an oyster and a slice of coppa colla, then pop under a very hot grill for about 1 minute. Serve one half shell per person as a starter.

Beef, Oyster and Christmas Ale Pudding

You will need a good old-fashioned 2-pint pudding basin for this, plus some greaseproof paper and some string.

ingredients

225g suet pastry (see page 194)
500g braising steak, trimmed
   and cut into small bite-sized
   pieces (Keep the trimmings)
2 onions, finely diced
2 carrots, evenly diced
1 clove garlic, finely diced
2 bay leaves
pinch of sugar
100ml red wine
200ml Christmas Ale, brewed
   locally by Shepherd Neame
300ml chicken stock
18 Whitstable Rocky oysters
50g plain flour
cayenne, salt, pepper, knob
   of butter
30ml olive oil

Sieve the flour with the salt and cayenne. Coat the meat evenly with the flour mixture, dusting away any excess. Put the oil into a pan and brown the meat in batches until it is all sealed. Put the browned meat to one side.

In a separate pan, sweat the onions in a little oil and butter, together with the bay leaf. Add a pinch of sugar, plus salt and pepper, and allow the onions to caramelise until they're golden. In another pan, sweat the carrots in some oil until tender and add the garlic. Now place the carrot mixture and the meat into the pan with the onions. Add the ale, and keep just simmering until the liquid has reduced to virtually nothing.

Retrieve the pan you cooked the beef in and reheat until it's very hot. Add the red wine, scraping the bottom of the pan as you do so. Sieve the red wine on to the meat mixture, add the stock, bring to a nice simmer and cook for an hour to an hour and a half until the meat is tender. Turn off the heat and allow the meat mixture to go cold.

While the meat is cooking, make the suet paste. Roll it out and line a 2-pint pudding basin leaving enough paste for a lid. Put the bowl with the paste into the fridge and allow it to rest for 10 to 15 minutes.

Once the meat mixture and the paste are cold, open the oysters, reserving the liquor. Add the liquor to the meat mixture and mix well, then place in the pudding basin, dispersing the oysters evenly every now and then until you've used them all up.

Cover the pudding with the suet paste lid, seal with your fingers, then cover with silicone paper, pleating the top to allow it room to expand. Tie with string, then cover the whole lot with foil. Place in a steamer and steam for 2 hours. Remember to make sure the saucepan doesn't boil dry. If you have any gravy or liquor left, warm it gently in a pan and serve on the side as extra gravy.

Forestière Oysters

This is a wonderful and unusual mixture of flavours devised by oyster lover and writer Shirley Line.

ingredients

Serves 4

32 Whitstable Rocky oysters
500g fresh button mushrooms
100g shallots, finely chopped
juice of 1 lemon
2 tbsp parsley, finely chopped
4 tbsp of crème fraiche
100g Gruyère cheese,
   finely grated
freshly ground black pepper
knob of butter

Open the oysters, save the liquor and arrange them out of their shells in a shallow flameproof serving dish. Clean the mushrooms by wiping them with kitchen paper. (Never wash mushrooms, they absorb the water.) Chop them very finely. Melt the butter in a frying pan, add the shallots and sauté for 1 minute. Stir in the mushrooms and lemon juice and cook for another minute. Add the oyster liquor with the black pepper to taste. Then stir in the parsley and the crème fraiche. Spoon some sauce over each oyster and then sprinkle with a little of the grated Gruyère. Put the dish under a preheated hot grill until the cheese bubbles. Serve immediately.

Oyster Soup

ingredients

Serves 4

36 Whitstable rocky oysters
600ml fish stock (see page 188)
1 onion, finely diced
a quarter of fennel, diced
good knob of butter
100ml white wine
200ml double cream
salt, cayenne pepper and a
    squeeze of lemon juice

Sweat the onions in the butter for about 5 minutes until they're soft but still uncoloured, add the fennel and sweat for another 3 minutes. Add the wine and reduce until the pan is virtually dry.

Meanwhile, heat the fish stock and then add the hot stock to the onions. Return to a gentle simmer. Open 24 of the oysters, retaining as much liquor as possible and add the oysters and liquor to the pan. Simmer for another 8 minutes. Add a squeeze of lemon juice and a good pinch of cayenne. Then place in a food mixer or blender until smooth, then pass through a sieve.

Return to a clean pan. Warm the cream and add to the soup. Simmer and check the seasoning. Check the consistency too – it should be thick enough to coat a spoon. Open the remaining oysters, add the liquor to the soup, then just before serving add the remaining oysters, allowing three per bowl.

the oyster seekers

Oysters are more beautiful than any religion ...
There's nothing in Christianity or Buddhism
that quite matches the unselfishness of an oyster.
SAKI (H H MUNRO)

Oyster Recipes from Another Age

Whitstable oysters are enjoying a renaissance but they have, of course, been enjoyed for centuries and cooks throughout the years have never tired of experimenting.

to fry oysters

Take a quarter of a Hundred of large Oysters, beat the yolks of two eggs, add to it a little nutmeg, and a blade of mace pounded, a spoonful of flour and a little salt, dip in oysters, and fry them in hog's lard [pig fat] light brown, if you choose you may add a little parsley shred fine. NB They are a proper garnish for cod's head, calf's head and most made dishes.

FROM *THE EXPERIENCED ENGLISH HOUSEKEEPER* BY MRS RAFFAULT 1769

Mrs Raffault trained as a cook at Arley Hall in Cheshire and married the gardener there in 1763. In the following 18 years she gave birth to 16 daughters. Yet she still managed to run a confectionery shop in Manchester, three Lancashire Inns and write her famous cookery book, which was reprinted thirteen times. Her cooking was delicious, her recipes superb and she was much admired.

to make oyster loaves

Take small French rasps or you may like to make little round loaves. Make a round hole in the top, scrape out all the crumbs, then put your oysters into a tossing pan with their liquor and crumbs that came out of your rasps or loaves and a good lump of butter. Stew them together five or six minutes, then put in a spoonful of good cream, fill your rasps or loaves, lay a bit of crust [the loaf lid] carefully on again. Set them in the oven to crisp. Three are enough for a side dish.

ANON,19TH CENTURY

Today, you might find that one or two are enough for a good lunch!

the oyster seekers

oyster toast

A la John Bailey

Bruise one small anchovy in a mortar fine, take a score of oysters, Whitstable Natives or Hampshire Royals are best and cast off their beards. Chop the oysters up finely, put anchovy and oysters into a small saucepan. Mix both together with sufficient cream to give it a pleasing consistency. Heat well over the fire [hob], stirring all the time. Spread on a round of buttered toast, baked crisp and crust cast off. Serve up hot in slices. Eat in solemn silence and wash down with a glass of brown sherry.

ANON, *LONDON AT TABLE* (1800s)

beefsteak and oyster sauce

Beef and oysters have often been served together in the past, in steak, kidney and oyster pies and puddings, and as a sauce like this. The sauce was also often served with fish.

Strain off the liquor from the oysters and throw them into cold water to take off the grit while you simmer the liquor with a bit of mace and lemon peel. Then put the oysters in, stew them a few minutes, add a little cream if you have it and some butter

rubbed in a little flour. Let them boil up once and have rumpsteaks well seasoned and broiled (grilled) ready for throwing the oyster sauce over the moment you are to serve.

MRS RUNDELL, *A NEW SYSTEM OF DOMESTIC COOKERY* (1806)

Mrs Rundell was born in Shropshire and married Thomas Rundell, a jeweller, from Ludgate Hill in London. She was in her early sixties when she wrote this book, and claimed she wrote it for the 'edification of her own daughters and their guidance upon marriage'. It was published anonymously by an old friend of the family, John Murray, and was immensely successful. Five to ten thousand copies were sold yearly. Mrs Rundell never asked for money and when, in 1809, Murray eventually sent her a cheque for £150, she said not to give her any more payment as the book had been a gift. Inevitably Murray became rich, although many people imitated Mrs Rundell's style and plagiarised her recipes. Eventually she accused Murray of neglecting her books. The fight ended up in court, when Mrs Rundell was in her late seventies. She was awarded £1,000 plus costs by the court. She died a few years later when she was 83.

oyster soup

It's interesting to compare the oyster soup of Soyer in 1846 to Mark and Delia's recipe of 2003. Soyer's taste was spicier, the Wheelers recipe more subtle, allowing through more of the oyster flavour. Mark and Delia are also more generous with the oysters but less with the salt.

Blanch 24 oysters until rather firm (they must not nearly boil), drain them in a sieve, save the liquor in which they were blanched. Put 2oz of butter into a stewpan. When it is melted, mix with it 3oz flour, stir it over a low fire [on hob] a short time. Afterwards let it cool then add the liquor of the oysters, a pint of milk, half a teaspoon of salt, a pinch of cayenne pepper, three peppercorns, a small piece of mace [quarter blade], a dessert-spoonful of Harvey sauce, and a teaspoon of essence of anchovy. Strain it through a tammie [muslin], boil it again ten minutes, skim well. Beard the oysters and put them in the tureen, add a couple of spoonfuls of cream to the soup when it is served and pour over the oysters.

MONSIEUR ALEXIS SOYER, CHEF OF THE REFORM CLUB, LONDON, THE GASTRONOMIC REGENERATOR (1846)

By the time he was 27 Alexis Soyer, who had come to England from France when he was 21, was a famous chef working at the equally famous Reform Club. He was described as a dandy, a comic-opera Frenchman and by the time he reached the Reform he had cooked for the Prince de Polignac and the English Duke of Cambridge, plus many grand families in many grand houses. But it was his post at the Reform Club that brought him recognition. His Cutlets à la Reform are still remembered, and on Queen Victoria's Coronation Day in June 1839, he cooked a sumptuous breakfast for two thousand aristocratic guests.

He left the Reform to open his own restaurant in Kensington in 1850, hoping that the Great Exhibition in the Park nearby would bring in the customers. Sadly, it didn't and he lost £7,000.

By 1855 the Crimean War was at its height and Soyer volunteered to go out there at his own expense to advise on diets and catering in military hosipitals. It's been said that he was to cooking in the Crimea what Florence Nightingale was to nursing, and he knew her well. Within a short time he had changed the hospital food out of all recognition, making soups and stews out of army rations that were actually palatable to the sick soldiers. He invented the field kitchen and a pot which kept tea hot. His diaries were full of affectionate accounts of Florence at work, on horseback and even under fire. He reorganised the victualling of the hospitals with her and she was full of praise for him.

He returned to England in 1857 and never received official thanks for his work. He died a year later, aged 48.

Oysters often pop up in literature. The famous Lewis Carroll poem 'The Walrus and the Carpenter' is a favourite:

The Walrus and the Carpenter
Were walking close at hand;
They wept like anything to see
Such quantities of sand:
'If this were only cleared away,'
They said, 'it would be grand!'

'If seven maids with seven mops
Swept it for half a year,
Do you suppose,' the Walrus said,
'That they could get it clear?'
'I doubt it,' said the Carpenter,
And shed a bitter tear.

But four young Oysters hurried up,
All eager for the treat;
Their shoes were clean and neat –
And this was odd, because, you know
They hadn't any feet.

'The time has come,' the Walrus said,
'To talk of many things:
Of shoes and ships and sealing wax
Of cabbages and kings
And why the sea is boiling hot
And whether pigs have wings.'
'A loaf of bread,' the Walrus said,
'Is what we chiefly need:
Pepper and vinegar besides
Are very good indeed –
Now if you're ready, Oysters dear,
We can begin to feed.'

The Carpenter said nothing but
'The butter's spread too thick!'
'I weep for you,' the Walrus said:
'I deeply sympathize.'
With sobs and tears he sorted out
Those of the largest size,
Holding his pocket-handkerchief
Before his streaming eyes.

But answer came there none –
And this was scarcely odd because
They'd eaten every one.

CHAPTER 2

Mussels, Cockles, Scallops and Clams

mussels

The humble mussel, with its beautiful blue-black shell and succulent, orangey, sweet flesh has, like the oyster, been consumed by the British for hundreds of years and also, like the oyster, has come in and out of fashion.

IIn the late 1800s, Whitstable people and visitors from London loved their mussels. Then, towards the end of the 1800s, there were bad floods rapidly followed by a harsh freezing winter. Times in the town were hard, just as they were in many fishing communities along England's coastline. The boats couldn't make it out to sea and things got so bad in Whitstable that a local well-to-do family set up a soup kitchen in the centre of town. The women of the town were, as ever, industrious. With little or no money for food, they headed for the beach and hunted for their 'shopping' there – picking mussels where they could find them and bringing them home for the evening meal. This gave birth to what was called Longrock Pudding, so-named because the mussels were often picked from a local beach towards Herne Bay called The Longrock. This was a kind of mussel steamed pudding, which was basic but nutritious, hot and, most importantly, filling. The mussels gave protein, the suet crust carbohydrate and a simple white sauce made with the mussel liquor and a little onion added flavour. Parsley could be added for colour, and vegetables, if you could find any, added to the goodness.

By the Twenties, most reasonably affluent young people wouldn't eat mussels; they were 'poor' food, associated with earlier, hard times, when their mothers had to go scavenging on the beach for sustenance. It wasn't until after the Second World War that families heading for the Kent coast on holiday rediscovered mussels, eaten cooked and cold with lashings of malt vinegar. But, even when the mussel was spurned as a source of food, mussels were still useful. The fishermen used them as ballast in the sailing ships and light barges that crossed the Channel to fish off the coast of Belgium and France. It was a very sensible idea: bobbing about on the choppy Channel was no fun in these light craft, so the men filled the hold with mussels. Once they reached their fishing grounds they emptied the mussels into the sea, fished and brought their catch back home in the now empty hold. As a result, many of the mussels you tuck into in Northern France and Belgium probably originated in Whitstable a few generations ago.

The French and the Belgians have always been keen on mussel-stew. In Belgium they add big chunks of carrot and celery. In France they add white wine and lots of garlic, onions and parsley. In Britain we stuck to malt vinegar on the whole until the Sixties when people discovered foreign travel – and French Moules Marinière. After that, in the Seventies, moules became chic once again and were a must of the sophisticated menu. Now they are almost standard and, as in Normandy where they

use local Armagnac to add flavour, we use Kentish apple cider to add flavour to the traditional mussel stew. Apples and mussels go together very nicely.

You can still hunt for your own mussels at beaches all over England. In Whitstable there are mussel banks off Whitstable and Seasalter and they're especially good in the small bays between Margate and Birchington. But they are usually quite small and then there is the chitter problem – a chitter is a barnacle. The chitters don't affect the fish, but they do house mud and grit and they're tenacious little things. They will hang on for all they are worth, coming off only in the heat of cooking, thus ruining your beautiful wine or cider sauce and giving diners an unwelcome taste of the beach.

Mussels have little sticky pads with which to attach themselves to rocks, and you need to debeard them – get out the bits of weed – before you cook them, or 'get the hairy man out', as they used to say. In other words, gathering and cooking mussels yourself can be hard work – so be prepared to scrub. They must be tightly shut – the mussel must be cooked alive. Any that are open are dead and must be thrown away. Even so a tightly shut mussel can fool you if you've picked it yourself – it may open up to reveal merely a load of grit, sealed by mud. And that's your sauce gone.

picking your own mussels

Mussels are good and plentiful around the British coast but remember that they like cool, living water so in Whitstable we advise not picking them in the summer when the mussels are spawning and the water is warm and more polluted. Wherever you are, avoid mussels that have attached themselves to anything iron such as old anchors or other people's rubbish – they won't taste good and may not do you any good either. Remember the golden rules: clean thoroughly – or buy those ready cleaned and scrubbed – and discard any that are open when you get them or don't open when cooked and discard any that float in water when you clean them. In the restaurant we sometimes serve local mussels if someone has managed to pick up some good ones which aren't too small or too chittery, but usually, as we serve them all year round, we go for Scottish mussels that are rope-grown, i.e. cultivated up ropes and kept in flowing – not stagnant – water. Even so we still get the odd chitter.

Nowadays you can buy mussels ready prepared with garlic butter or sauce in supermarkets – but these will never give the satisfaction of cooking mussels bought live from a good fish-monger or a restaurant like Wheelers. Even if you get them from the fish-monger, give them another good wash before you cook them, discard any that are open before cooking and discard any that refuse to open after cooking.

Ideally you should get your mussels on the day you're going to cook them. They like the cool and the damp, so put them in a bucket and cover it with damp newspaper. They don't much like the fridge, although they will survive in the fridge overnight. Delia much laments the passing of the old-fashioned, well-ventilated cool larder which all fish seem to love. Not hot, not warm but cool and airy. In the old days they used to put the mussels in a bucket of water in the larder and sprinkle a bit of oatmeal over the water. The oatmeal irritated the mussel, which forced it to spit out anything that shouldn't be in there, like grit. You can't do this for too long, though (perhaps 3 or 4 hours), because there's not much oxygen in tap water – it's 'still' water and rapidly becomes 'dead' water. You can keep your scrubbed and clean, but uncooked, mussels in a bucket of water sprinkled with some salt but, again, only for 3 or 4 hours at most.

Once you're ready to cook your mussels – already cleaned and scrubbed – it couldn't be easier. Take a pan with a tight lid, add a little olive oil to the hot pan, along with a few herbs, add some cider or wine, then put in the mussels and let them steam for a few minutes only. Give them a stir after about 3 minutes when they're starting to open. What you want are mussels that aren't overcooked – they go a bit rubbery if you're not careful – and if they're undercooked they're too squidgy. Take one out and test it. If it feels soft and 'well-sprung', you've hit the spot. Learn by trial and error and you'll always be able to produce a delicious, filling meal in minutes. Serve with lots of fresh, crusty bread to soak up the juices.

Moules Marinière

Everyone has their own version of Moules Marinière – this is ours.

ingredients

Serves 4

2 medium onions, finely diced
1 medium shallot, finely diced
2 cloves of garlic, chopped
2 tbsp flat leaf parsley
   (reserve the stalks)
1.5kg live mussels, cleaned
   and debearded
juice of half a lemon
200ml dry white wine
150ml fish stock
1 tbsp butter

Sweat the onions, shallots and parsley stalks in a pan. Don't allow them to brown, but merely soften. Then add the stock and the wine and cook for 2 minutes. Bring to the boil and simmer for 5 minutes. Add the mussels to the pan until they have steamed open – discard any that remain shut. Remove the mussels and divide between four plates. Squeeze the lemon juice into the stock. Remove the parsley stalks, add the chopped parsley, a good knob of butter and some salt and pepper. Bring back to the boil and spoon over the mussels. Serve immediately with warm, crusty bread.

the oyster seekers

the oyster seekers

Rope-Grown Mussels Steamed with Apple and Cider

ingredients

Serves 4

2kg of Scottish rope-grown
    mussels
half a carrot, finely diced
a quarter of a leek, finely diced
1 Cox's apple, finely diced
juice of half a lemon
1 shallot finely diced
1 garlic clove, finely diced
200ml dry cider
200ml double cream
mixed herbs, salt, pepper,
    cayenne, olive oil and a good
    knob of butter

Place the shallot, garlic, carrot, leek and apple into a hot pan with a little olive oil and sweat for five minutes without browning. Add the mussels and cider, put a lid on the pan and steam gently for a few minutes until the mussels open.

Divide the mussels between four bowls, leaving the vegetables in the pan. Turn the heat back up to boiling point then add the cream, lemon juice, cayenne, a knob of butter and the herbs. Stir continuously and as soon as the sauce is ready pour over the mussels. Finish with a twist of black pepper and serve immediately.

Martha's Mussels with Suet Crust

This is Martha, Delia's mother's, version of The Longrock Pudding.

ingredients

Serves 4

300ml milk
2kg live mussels, debearded
   and washed
a clove
1 onion
1 bay leaf
150ml white wine
1 shallot, finely diced
1 clove garlic, finely diced
a quarter of a carrot, finely diced
a quarter of leek, finely diced
a stick of celery, finely diced
olive oil
2 tbsp chopped parsley
1 tbsp chopped chives
56g flour
56g butter
squeeze of lemon
cayenne

FOR THE SUET CRUST:
112g self-raising flour
56g suet – from the butcher
   or the supermarket
half a red onion, finely diced
a few sprigs of thyme, leaves
   only (no stalks)
salt
4–6 tbsp cold water

First, make the suet pastry by sieving the flour and salt together, then adding the suet, onion, thyme leaves and finally the water, until you have a good, firmish dough. Stud the other onion with the clove and add that, with the bay leaf, to the milk in a pan. Bring to the boil, simmer for 5 minutes, then allow to cool.

Sweat the shallot, garlic, carrot, leek and celery in another pan with some oil until they're soft but not browned. Then add the mussels and the wine. After the mussels have steamed open, remove them from their shells and put to one side. Pass the liquor through a sieve and put that to one side.

Melt the butter in another pan, add the flour, stirring to form a roux and cook out, stirring constantly for a couple of minutes, taking care not to let it brown. Gradually add the cooled stock and the milk and cook gently for about 20 minutes until you have a rich, mussely sauce.

Roll out the suet pastry to about ¾cm thick and, using a saucer, cut out four discs. Steam these on a plate over some boiling water for 15 minutes. Finish the sauce by gently reheating and adding the parsley, chives, lemon juice and cayenne. Add the mussels until just hot. Divide the mussel mixture between the plates and put a suet crust disc on top of each one. Serve immediately.

cockles

Walk along the mud flats of East Kent at low tide and you can see where the cockles are. They bury themselves deep in the mud but give themselves away by their tiny blowholes. Whereas the lugworms throw up wormcasts, and clams and razor fish – or 'spooks' as they're known – give bigger blowholes; the tiny blowholes are cockles all right.

Whitstable boasts some of the best cockles in the world – sweet and succulent. Many find their way to Spain to be pickled in vinegar or brine, then they're shipped back to Wales to be packed and then distributed worldwide. Some even come back to Whistable to be sold in jars! You can pick your own if you're prepared to dig in the mud. Delia knows of a wonderful cockle 'larder' not so far from Whitstable but she's not saying where.

In France, cockles are sold alive to be thrown into soups and stews. You can also buy them live here but we tend to eat them cooked. Unlike mussels, cockles are cooked at the harbour as soon as they have landed. In the East Kent area the cockle season is from June to December and that's when you get the best ones, fresh off the boats. They are dredged up into the hold with a kind of enormous vacuum cleaner; when they reach shore they are unloaded at the harbour by crane; then they are taken by lorry to the cockle shed, where they're immediately cooked in boiling water. Then they go up a conveyor belt, through another wash like a spin dryer and then through a hot 'copper'. A copper is a large metal container, which can hold between 5 and 15 gallons of water and cockles. Nowadays it is heated by gas or electricity, but in the old days it would have been heated using coal. The cockles are steamed in the copper and then it's into another washing plant – still in their shells. After that they go into a giant sieve, where they're separated from their shells, then another wash, then another wash – and finally into ice-cold water to cool. The cockle's life after catching is far from uneventful.

The cockle with a good bit of malt vinegar has always been a favourite at the seaside. Some people swear by cockle sandwiches – try it, using brown bread and butter, white pepper and very little malt vinegar and you'll probably be hooked. In the early part of the last century cockles, like mussels, were regarded as cheap, poor food but anyone who lived by the sea always realised that they were nutritious as well as free. Cockle cake used to be common. Grease a cake tin and sprinkle in breadcrumbs, mix a couple of eggs with half a pint or so of milk, add however many cockles you want, add salt and pepper and bake in the oven in a baking tray of water until the 'cake' is set. Slice and eat warm; tasty and nutritious – and cheap.

Cockles can also be used to good effect in sauces and soups. Add some (unvinegared) cockles to a thinnish white sauce with some Vermouth and parsley and you have the perfect sauce for cod. Serve with mashed potato and fresh green veg. These days at Wheelers we use cockles quite frequently in pasta and included here are some of the most popular dishes.

Cockle and Herb Linguine

ingredients

Serves 4

500g live cockles
olive oil
1 bunch of flat leaf parsley,
    stalks on
2 medium shallots, finely diced
2 cloves of garlic, finely diced
450g fresh linguine
150ml double cream
3 plum tomatoes, blanched,
    skinned, de-seeded and diced
100ml white wine
half a bunch of picked chervil
1 tsp mixed peppercorns,
    cayenne, juice of one lime

Place the cockles in a bowl, cover with water and wash thoroughly, changing the water three times. Put the olive oil into a deep saucepan and add the shallot and garlic, parsley stalks and mixed peppercorns. Allow to sweat for a few minutes, ensuring that the mixture does not brown.

Put the drained cockles into a pan with the white wine, cover with a lid and allow cockles to steam open. Discard any that don't open after 5 minutes of heating. Put the open cockles into a bowl. Then place the cockle juice and wine mixture into a clean pan and bring to the boil with the lime juice, cream and cayenne, and allow to thicken slightly.

Place the pasta into a pan of boiling water and cook until al dente. While the pasta is cooking – this should take 2 or 3 minutes – remove the cockles from their shells, keeping a few shells for decoration. When the pasta is cooked, drain, put it into the cream sauce, and add the cockles, parsley and chervil along with the tomato. Mix thoroughly and serve immediately with a few cockles in their shells for decoration.

Cockle and Clam Risotto

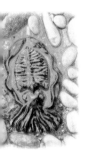

Constant stirring is the secret of a good risotto. Always use a wooden spoon – not a metal one – and always use risotto rice.

ingredients

Serves 4

1kg cockles
1kg live clams
2 medium shallots, finely diced
1 clove of garlic, peeled and
    chopped
knob of butter
bunch of chives, finely chopped
225g Arborio rice
1.5 tbsp grated Parmesan
lemon juice
half a bulb of fennel – core
    removed – finely diced
1 dessertspoon of mascarpone
    cheese
400ml white wine
200ml chicken stock, if needed
2 bay leaves and a quarter of a
    bunch of chervil, picked over

Put the cockles and clams in separate bowls and wash both in three changes of water. Place in separate pans over a medium heat. Place a bay leaf and 200ml of the white wine into each pan. Cover and boil so the cockles and clams steam open. When they're cooked, after 5 minutes, remove them from the pans, immediately discarding any that haven't opened. Put the cockles and clams to one side. Strain both lots of cooking liquor into one pan, put back on to the heat to simmer and add the chicken stock. Remove the cockles and clams from their shells.

In a thick-bottomed pan melt the butter, add the diced shallots and garlic and allow to sweat for 3 minutes without browning. Add the rice and allow it to go translucent, which should take about a minute. Add the hot stock one ladle at a time, stirring continuously. Keep adding the stock until the rice is just nice and tender.

To finish, fold in the clams and cockles along with the Parmesan and Mascarpone cheeses. Adjust the seasoning to taste and serve immediately. Add a squeeze of lemon juice and decorate with the chopped chives and chervil.

Cockle Recipes from Another Age

roast leg of mutton with cockles

Make cuts all over the leg of mutton (or lamb) with a pointed knife and into each of these stuff a freshly cooked shelled cockle (not the kind pickled in brine or vinegar which are too strong) rather as if the meat were larded with them. Roast it as usual and serve it garnished with horseradish.

MRS GLASSE, *THE ART OF COOKERY MADE PLAIN AND EASY* (1747)

Mrs Hannah Glasse's book was so popular that it was still being reprinted in 1843, nearly 100 years later. Her recipes were not intended for chefs in restaurants or cooks in great houses but aimed to be understood by servants. She was plain-speaking, set everything out clearly and concentrated on good English cooking. She is believed to have lived in Covent Garden, London, and she had no time for 'fancy', French cooking. In one of her books, in a chapter for 'Seafaring Men', she writes:

If I have not wrote in the high polite Stile, I hope I shall be forgiven; for my intention is to instruct the lower Sort: and therefore must treat them in their own way ... in many Things in cookery the great cooks have such a high way of expressing themselves that the poor girls are at a loss to know what they mean and all Receipt Books yet printed there are such an odd jumble of things as would quite spoil a good dish and indeed some things so extravagant that it would be almost a shame to make use of them when a dish can be made as good, or better, without them.

Mrs Glasse has also been attributed with the famous cookery quote: 'First catch your hare ...' In fact what she actually wrote was: 'Take your hare when it is cased [gutted].' The former quote has since been blamed on an imaginative tabloid journalist of the day!

welsh cockle pie

Cook one quart of cockles in a cup of water only long enough for the shells to open. Line the sides only of the pie dish with thickly rolled pastry. Put a layer of shelled cockles in the bottom of the dish. Sprinkle these with chopped spring onions or chopped

chives then add a layer of diced fat bacon. Repeat these layers until the dish is full then pour in the strained liquid in which the cockles were boiled, adding pepper. Cut fairly thin strips of pastry and with these make a criss cross over the pie. Cook slowly until the pastry is done.

SHEILA HUTCHINS, *ENGLISH RECIPES AND OTHERS FROM ENGLAND, SCOTLAND, WALES AND IRELAND, AS THEY APPEARED IN EIGHTEENTH AND NINETEENTH CENTURY COOK BOOKS*

Sheila Hutchins was a famous cookery writer of the 1960s, 70s and 80s, who felt that, 'English cooking had been in a decline for so long that people have almost forgotten how good it once was.' Sheila did her best to change all that. She was fascinated by old recipe books and studied hundreds. She wrote books of her own and, for many years, was a daily columnist for the *Daily Express*. She died some years ago. People who worked with her at the *Express* remember her as an extraordinary, large and impressive lady, totally professional in her work and totally passionate about English cooking.

This cockle pie she adapted from an old Welsh recipe and said it was delicious served hot with new potatoes or cold with salad and a creamy dressing. She writes that in some Welsh villages they used to make limpet pies the same way but would add sliced onion and chopped hard-boiled egg.

scallops and clams

Oysters, like clams, love the Thames estuary, where they can lie and flourish inshore and snooze in the mud. They like the lack of salt in the water. Unfortunately scallops, which for many are almost as good, love salt, so the inshore waters won't do for them. To catch our scallops the local fishermen usually go further afield, fishing in the Channel and along the south coast off Rye and Folkstone. Like oysters they lie on the mud but if the mud is soft they will bury themselves down a little perhaps as deep as an inch or so.

Local scallops are seasonal. They start what's called 'tonguing up' around November/December, which means that they start to develop their roe or coral, and they're ready to be fished come the end of January through until March and April – the summer months are best for good fresh scallops.

Like oysters, they should be tightly closed if you buy them alive, although it's better to buy them ready cleaned, as often when you open a live scallop you'll find that it has a high percentage of mud and grit. Here at Wheelers we get them live locally – from Rye, as Whitstable water isn't salty enough – and clean and cook them on the premises. Mark removes the white, and some poor soul (usually Delia) has to sort the roe from the frill, the mantle and the fin and the rest of the mud. What you should be left with is the white flesh and the orange roe. The rest can be discarded.

But they are a very special shellfish and a few go a long way. Just throw a few pieces of good streaky bacon in a pan until the fat runs, adding perhaps a little butter and some bread to make fried bread. When the bread is fried and the bacon almost crispy, place your scallops in the pan. Cook for just a couple more minutes, giving the pan the odd shake, and serve with a good wedge of lemon and maybe a little black pepper. The perfect meal.

Or you can be more adventurous. The scallop takes well to sauces and can be complemented by a variety of flavours. Here are some of the dishes we create for the restaurant if you want to spend a little more time. And there's always the famous Coquilles St Jacques, which may be out of fashion just now but is easy to cook, always delicious and always impressive.

the oyster seekers

the oyster seekers

Scallops have their own patron saint – St James the apostle, the brother of John. James was, originally, of course, a fisherman and used the scallop shell as his emblem, which is why crusaders of the order of St James later adopted the shell as their symbol. Legend has it that, after James was martyred, the boat carrying his body landed on the coast of Spain causing a horse on shore to bolt into the sea with its rider. Both disappeared beneath the waves for a considerable time – then miraculously rose to the surface covered in scallop shells. During the Middle Ages, the scallop shell was also worn by pilgrims to his shrine in Compostela in Galicia, Spain. Churches all over Europe devoted to the saint are frequently adorned with the shell emblem. In Marylebone, London, you can see some beautiful examples at St James's Roman Catholic Church.

So it's no wonder the French named their famous creamy scallop dish Coquilles St Jacques after the saint – it's divine.

Glazed Coquilles St Jacques

ingredients

Serves 4

12 scallops, shucked, with their
corals – keep four shells
500g potatoes, peeled and
quartered
150ml double cream
1 medium shallot, finely diced
100ml white wine
100ml fish stock
50ml Noilly Prat
a few parsley stalks
bay leaf
2 tbsp chopped parsley
28g butter
28g flour
4 tbsp grated Pecorino, a delicious
medium-soft Italian cheese
juice of a half a lemon
1 packet of rocket
2 strips of pancetta, cut into
lardons
knob of butter

Boil the potatoes in salted water until tender. Drain thoroughly and return to the pan to dry briefly, then pass through a fine sieve. Warm the cream and add to the potatoes along with the knob of butter and chopped parsley. Adjust the seasoning and then put into a piping bag with a star-shaped nozzle. Wash the scallops thoroughly and dry. Lightly grease each of the four scallop shells with butter. Neatly pipe a border of potato around each shell. Place the wine, Noilly Prat and stock into a pan along with the diced shallot, parsley stalks and bay leaf. Bring to the boil and simmer for 5 minutes.

Wilt the rocket in a hot pan with a little butter for a minute, drain and divide between the four shells. Fry the lardons in a little oil until just crispy but still tender. Dry them on kitchen paper and add to the shells.

Put the scallops and their corals into the wine mixture and quickly bring back to the boil. Remove immediately, cut the scallops in half widthways, and put three pieces plus the roes into each shell.

Next, make a roux by melting the butter and adding the flour in a pan, stirring constantly. Gradually add the strained cooking liquor until the sauce coats the back of the spoon. Allow to cook gently for 20 minutes. Season with salt and pepper and simmer for 5 minutes. Add the lemon juice and the remaining cream, then pour over the scallops in the shells. Grate the pecarino over the shells and place in a baking tray. Bake in the oven for 10 minutes until golden brown or quickly put them under a hot grill. Serve at once.

the oyster seekers

A Papillotte of Shellfish and Linguine with Coconut, Lime Leaf, Coriander and Fresh Ginger

ingredients

Serves 4

500g mussels
500g clams
500g cockles
8 raw tiger prawns
4 whole lemon grass
8 lime leaves
1 tin of coconut milk
1 tsp fresh ginger, finely diced
1 small red chilli, finely diced
30g butter
100ml white wine
200ml fish stock
4 spring onions, finely diced
225g fresh linguine
1 tbsp lightly chopped coriander

Debeard, wash and clean the mussels, cockles and clams. Make the papillottes following the diagram opposite. Grease the centre of the foil with butter. Place a piece of lemon grass and a lime leaf on each.

Take the fresh linguine, put in boiling salted water for 2 to 3 minutes, remove, refresh in cold water, then drain. Put the linguine in a bowl and add the ginger, chilli, coriander and spring onions, lightly season and mix evenly. Divide the pasta between the four pieces of foil/greaseproof and add the cockles, mussels, clams and prawns. Lightly fold up the sides of the foil and greaseproof which surrounds your seapod to form a small lip.

Next, divide the wine, stock and coconut milk between the four mounds. Fold over the other half of the foil and greaseproof so that all the edges meet. Seal the edges by twisting them and working all around forming a bag.

Place in a preheated oven for 15 to 18 minutes. The bag will 'blow up' as steam is created within it. Put each bag on a plate and serve, cutting the bag open at the table so you can really appreciate the lovely fresh aromas.

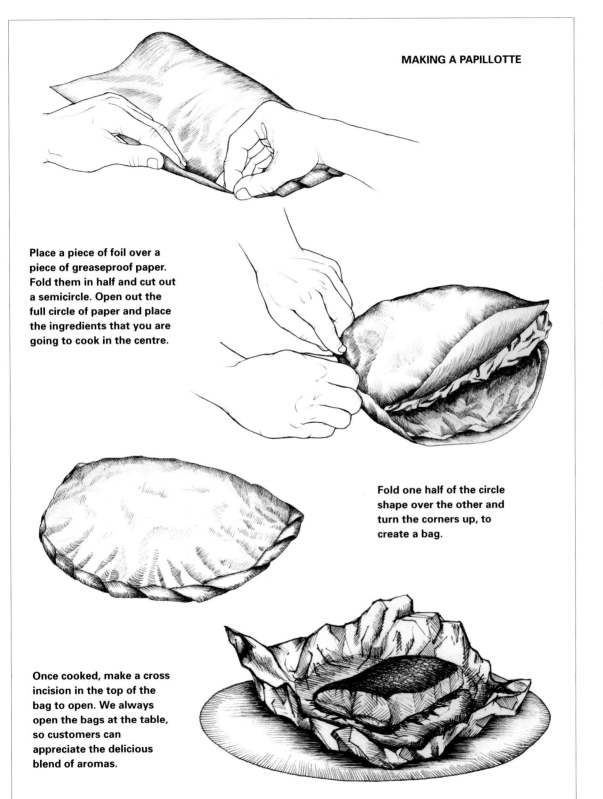

MAKING A PAPILLOTTE

Place a piece of foil over a piece of greaseproof paper. Fold them in half and cut out a semicircle. Open out the full circle of paper and place the ingredients that you are going to cook in the centre.

Fold one half of the circle shape over the other and turn the corners up, to create a bag.

Once cooked, make a cross incision in the top of the bag to open. We always open the bags at the table, so customers can appreciate the delicious blend of aromas.

Clam Chowder

ingredients

Serves 4

2 sticks of celery, diced
1 medium white onion, diced
the white of one leek, diced
450g potatoes, peeled and grated
900g Palade clams – local clams,
    bigger than a cockle, but smaller
    than a whelk
a few sprigs of thyme
150ml white wine
100ml fish stock (see page188)
2 plum tomatoes, peeled,
    deseeded and diced
8 rashers of bacon cut into
    1cm lardons
additional fish stock (if needed)
100ml milk
75ml double cream
salt, pepper, squeeze of lemon,
    olive oil

Heat some oil in a pan big enough to make your soup, then add the bacon and cook until crispy. Remove the bacon with a slotted spoon and drain through a colander, but keep the bacon fat in the pan. Add the onion to the pan and sweat for a few minutes – don't brown – then add the celery, leek and potato and sweat for 5 minutes. Meanwhile, put the wine and stock in another pan, add the clams and cook until they've steamed open. Remove and drain the clams. Strain the cooking liquor left in the pan through muslin. The quantity of liquid required is 1.5 litres so, if there is shortfall, add some fish stock. Add this stock to the vegetables, bring to boil and simmer for 15 minutes, then add the thyme.

Remove the clams from their shells, put in a bowl, cover with a little stock and, when they have cooled, leave them in the fridge until needed. Blend the chowder in a food processor or with a blender. Add the cream and milk, return to the boil and simmer for 5 minutes. Adjust the seasoning and add a squeeze of lemon juice. Reheat the clams in their stock then add them to the soup with the bacon pieces. Serve piping hot. A few clam shells can be added for decoration.

the oyster seekers

Opposite: **Clams love the Thames Estuary**

the oyster seekers

A Salad of Scallops Served with Roasted Ceps, Asparagus, Sun-Dried Tomatoes and Parmesan Crisps

ingredients

Serves 4

12 medium scallops with roes
225g sliced raw ceps
4 slices Parma ham
mixed salad leaves
12 spears of asparagus
70g grated Parmesan
100g sun-dried tomatoes
a few sprigs of chervil
a few fresh tarragon leaves
4 tbsp balsamic vinegar,
  plus 8 tbsp olive oil
4 additional tbsp olive oil

Ask your fishmonger to clean the scallops and keep the roes. Wash them again when you get them home and dry on kitchen paper. Trim the ceps with a sharp knife and slice finely. Place in a hot pan with a little oil and cook until golden. Peel and cook the asparagus in boiling water, then refresh in cold water. Cut the Parma ham into even pieces and grill until crispy, turning once. Take a clean non-stick pan and lightly sprinkle with Parmesan until melted. Carefully remove from the pan with a palette knife and place over a rolling pin, making a curved biscuit. Allow to cool. Mix the chervil and tarragon with the salad leaves. Make a dressing with the vinegar, whisked with the olive oil and some salt and pepper. Season the scallops and pan-fry in a little oil until golden, turning once – this takes about 2 minutes. Add a squeeze of lemon juice.

To serve, dress the salad leaves with the dressing, and put on individual plates. Add the warm ceps, the asparagus and tomatoes and finally the Parma ham, building up your salad to a peak in the middle. Arrange the scallops and the roes around the side and top with some of the Parmesan biscuit broken into pieces.

CHAPTER 3

Shrimps and Prawns

shrimps

You need patience to cope with shrimps – all that peeling – but they're well worth it.

There are brown shrimps and pink shrimps. You're unlikely to find the pink ones near to shore any more in East Kent, mainly because cod took to coming to the flats, and shrimps are their favourite meal. Men still fish for them in deeper waters off the Isle of Sheppey, though, and they really are delicious. So for pink shrimps you need to go to your fishmonger or harbour – or get a boat.

Brown shrimps – once never bothered with because the pink ones were deemed better – are still there and still plentiful on the tideline. To catch them, you'll need waders, a bucket and a big shrimping net, plus the time to walk up and down when the tide is really low. It will be worth it, though, as you should come home with enough shrimps for a good few teas and more. If you love the sea, doing this is an absolute pleasure, especially if you need to get away from it all or need a bit of thinking – or no-thinking –

time. The bonus is that, at the end of it, you get a wonderful delicious meal.

Fresh shrimps, especially the brown ones, aren't initially attractive; 'grotty, gery/brown things' Delia calls them. They're also translucent, like prawns, when raw. But they are delicious.

To cook them, put them in boiling hot water as soon as possible after catching. Boil for just a couple of minutes or so then take them out and spread them on a tray of some sort to dry naturally – that way the skin won't go soggy and they're easier to peel. Then peel and eat them.

Delia remembers being a small child when a local fisherman used to send his daughter along with half a gallon of shrimps for Sunday tea. She adores them, and by the age of four could peel them to perfection. Martha, her mother, refused to let her father and uncle have a cup of tea until they'd eaten all the shrimps on their plate – because they were usually so engrossed in the shrimps that the tea went cold. And that, of course, was a waste.

Delia still loves shrimps, but won't eat them until she's removed every last bit of leg. Others, one of them not a million miles away from this book, start peeling them thoroughly but then find they become so moreish that the legs and the body shell have to be munched as well. Mark prefers someone else to do the peeling and then he uses them in a variety of dishes.

Bob West's Shrimps

ingredients

Serves 2–3

2 pints fresh shrimps
half a gallon of water
2 dessertspoons table salt

Put the water and salt in a large pan and bring to the boil. Add the shrimps and allow the water to boil again. When the water becomes frothy, remove the shrimps from the water immediately.

Next – and this is important – spread your shrimps out on a perforated tray and allow to drain and dry naturally. If you don't have a perforated tray, put a piece of foil over an ordinary baking tray, puncture some holes in the foil and use that.

Once dry, eat as soon as possible – with brown bread and butter, a squeeze of lemon – or just on their own and still warm.

Potted Shrimps

ingredients

Serves 4

240g fresh brown shrimps, peeled
250g clarified butter
3 blades mace
a pinch of nutmeg
a pinch of cayenne

To clarify the butter, simply melt it, removing the fat that rises to the surface, then carefully pass it through muslin, leaving any fat behind.

Divide the shrimps into four pots or ramekins. Gently heat the clarified butter. Add the mace, cayenne and nutmeg. Allow the spices to infuse the butter. After 5 minutes, remove the mace and pour the butter over the shrimps, just enough to cover them, reserving any leftover butter. If there are any shrimps peeking out from the butter, add a little more. Allow to set.

The shrimps are now completely preserved and can be refrigerated. Serve with toast and lemon wedges and extra cayenne should anyone want it, although get them to taste the spicy butter first. Potted shrimps freeze well.

Brown Shrimp Omelette

When cooking an omelette, don't mix it too vigorously or you will beat the air out of it.

ingredients

2 whole eggs
1 egg, separated, with the white reserved
110g brown shrimps, peeled
knob of butter, cut into small cubes
splash of cream
salt and pepper

Crack the two whole eggs into a bowl. Add the third egg yolk, cream and the cubes of butter and mix together. Lightly fold in the shrimps to this mixture and season with salt and pepper. Lightly whisk the single egg white and fold into the shrimp mixture.

Take a small- to medium-sized non-stick pan and, when warmed on the stove, melt a good knob of butter in it. Pour in the egg mixture and mix carefully over a medium heat until almost cooked. Finish cooking the omelette by placing the pan under a grill.

Serve on a large plate, with a crisp salad and perhaps a few buttered new potatoes.

the oyster seekers

Brown Shrimp Sauce

The sauce can be used with a variety of plainly cooked fish. This amount is quite sufficient for six servings but, as the sauce can't be frozen and must be made with the rest of the meal, you have to adjust the amounts according to your needs.

ingredients

1 pint brown shrimps
2 tbsp brandy
2 pints fish stock (see page 188)
26g butter
salt and pepper to season
oil

Place the shrimps in a very hot oiled pan and toss around for about 3 minutes. Add the brandy and flambé by setting alight if possible – but do be careful you don't set yourself or the kitchen on fire.

Bring the fish stock to the boil in a separate pan then add the shrimps. Bring back to the boil and allow to simmer for about 8 minutes. Put the shrimp mixture into a food processor, in batches, blending until smooth. Pass the mixture through a fine sieve and then, if you really want to go to town, through muslin. Put the sauce back in the pan and bring back to the boil. Turn off the heat and whisk in the cold butter. Adjust the seasoning.

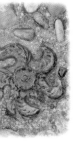

prawns

There's little to match a pile of prawns served with just a wedge of lemon, some brown bread and butter, and some good, strong, garlic mayonnaise for dipping – especially if you're eating them on a beach with the sun shining.

Prawns come in all shapes and sizes, depending on where they're caught. In Whitstable, come May time, you can put out little prawn traps – lobster pots on a miniature scale – and you might get lucky. But they do like cold water and as our waters warm up they head for the North Sea. Our fishermen get them in May and June – and sometimes in September too – but otherwise they come from off the shores of Norway and Sweden. You can always tell if prawns are local – really local: their shells are crisper and harder to peel when cooked.

Like all shellfish, prawns are very much individual in taste. Some people love to peel their own; some can't stand the thought of it, although it has to be said that those you peel yourself, or are freshly peeled for you, are really much tastier. The ready-peeled prawns we buy have had their skins blasted off by water. Then they're either frozen, put in salt water or left fresh, plain and chilled. Fresh and live prawns are a dirty pink/grey colour and translucent. When caught on the boats they are often boiled on board, immediately, forcing them to curl up as you would expect. It is a strange fact that prawns refuse to curl up until they're cooked, yet people would be surprised to see a straight prawn.

If you catch your own, or buy them fresh, boil them as soon as you can. They need only a few minutes in boiling salted water to get that lovely pink colour and you keep the flavour that way. If you're buying tiger prawns from the supermarket, or from your fishmonger – these are warm water or fresh water prawns – don't keep them for long once you get them home. Cook and use them as soon as possible – definitely that day.

Once you've got the knack, peeling a prawn is not difficult. First gently pinch off the hard tail skin. Take off the legs and unwrap the shell from the body. Then pull the flesh away from the head and eat, pausing perhaps to dip in a little garlic mayonnaise or vinegar.

King Prawn and Scallop Brochettes Skewered with Bay Sticks Served with a Tomato and Coriander Salsa

ingredients

Makes 4 brochettes

12 king prawns, raw, head-on
   but peeled
8 medium scallops
quarter of a bunch of coriander,
   picked over and chopped
   roughly
4 bay sticks, soaked briefly
   in water
4 plum tomatoes, blanched,
   deseeded and diced
1 medium shallot, finely diced
50ml white wine vinegar
olive oil
12 lemon segments
juice of 1 lime
salt and pepper
lemon wedges

Place the shallot, vinegar and coriander in a bowl. Season with salt and pepper. Fold in the diced tomatoes. Add the juice of one lime. Bind all these together with a little olive oil.

To make the brochettes, take the bay sticks – hopefully you can get them from a garden but if not use wooden skewers, in either case soak for half an hour in cold water before use – and skewer three prawns, two scallops and three lemon segments alternately on to each one, leaving more space at one end than the other. Season with salt and pepper and place in a hot oiled pan until golden brown on one side. Turn over and cook for a further 2 to 3 minutes until the fish is semi-firm to the touch.

Put the salsa on to individual plates and top with the warm brochettes. Finish with a lemon wedge and serve with a fresh, crisp salad. Eat immediately. This is a lovely dish for the barbecue.

the oyster seekers

Prawn and Dill Cocktail

ingredients

Serves 4

28 tiger prawns, raw, peeled
    and deveined
half a cos lettuce, finely shredded
a few mixed salad leaves
8 cherry tomatoes, cut in half
half a cucumber
6 tbsp good mayonnaise
2 tbsp tomato ketchup
1 tsp horseradish sauce
lemon juice
paprika, cayenne and Tabasco
8–10 fronds of freshly picked dill
4 lemon wedges
4 slices brown bread and butter
splash of brandy

Cook the prawns in boiling salted water for 2 to 3 minutes, drain and allow to cool, squeezing a little lemon juice over them while they're still warm. Using a mandolin, shred the cucumber into spaghetti-like strips (if you haven't got a mandolin cut into thin strips) and season with a little salt and pepper.

Mix together the mayonnaise, tomato ketchup, horseradish, lemon juice, a pinch of cayenne pepper and a splash each of Tabasco and brandy. Pick over the dill and snip into small pieces; fold into the sauce. Put the cucumber in a colander and allow any excess liquid to drain away. Mix together the cos lettuce and salad leaves then divide between four cocktail glasses. Top with some of the cucumber along with the cherry tomatoes. Arrange the prawns on top, then spoon over the sauce. Finish with a small pinch of paprika and serve with a lemon wedge each and brown bread with butter. Eat immediately.

Stir-Fried Prawns with Ginger, Coriander, Chilli and Bok Choi

ingredients

Serves 4

20 king prawns, raw, peeled,
  head on and deveined
4 bok choi
1 medium shallot, finely diced
a quarter of a bunch of coriander,
  picked over and chopped
1 clove of garlic, finely diced
1 piece of fresh ginger, peeled
  and cut into fine juliennes
2 spring onions, sliced thinly on
  the diagonal
sesame oil
juice of half a lime
light soy sauce
1 tbsp rice wine vinegar
1 small red chilli, finely diced
4 piquillo peppers, deseeded and
  finely sliced
1 courgette, cut into thin batons
a handful of cashew nuts

In a wok – or heavy pan, but a wok is best – sweat the shallots, garlic, chilli, ginger and spring onion in some sesame oil, ensuring that the mixture does not brown. Add the bok choi and courgette. Increase the heat and allow to wilt for 2 to 3 minutes. Sprinkle the finely sliced piquillo peppers on top and toss together. Season with salt and pepper. Add the rice wine vinegar, and the coriander, and mix thoroughly. Add the cashew nuts. Mix again.

Divide the warm salad between four plates. Clean the wok with some kitchen paper and reheat with a little more sesame seed oil. Stir-fry the prawns then put them on top of the vegetables. Squeeze over each plate a little lime juice, and add a little light soy sauce, and serve immediately.

Deep-Fried Dublin Bay Prawns Served with a Jersey Royal, Cep, Asparagus and Tomato Confit Salad

ingredients

Serves 4

16 large Dublin Bay prawns, live
300g small Jersey Royal potatoes
32 black olives, pitted
12 asparagus spears
6 tomatoes, blanched and peeled
4 tbsp cornflour
2 tbsp plain flour
3 little gem lettuces
4 medium ceps, cleaned
 and sliced
4 dessertspoon balsamic dressing
 (see recipe page 199)
a few sprigs of thyme and
 rosemary
2 cloves of garlic, thinly sliced
a little vinaigrette and a little
 olive oil
sea salt
½ tsp each of ginger, fourspice
 and coriander powder
ice-cold sparkling water

Put the prawns in boiling salted water and blanch for 1 minute. Remove and place in ice-cold water until cold. Remove immediately. Remove heads and carefully remove the shell. What should be left is a shell-less body with the tail piece still intact. Put the prawns on a tray, cover and put in the fridge. Gently scrub the potatoes and cook in boiling water until tender. Remove the Jerseys from the water, put in a bowl and pour over a little vinaigrette while they're still warm.

Peel and blanch the asparagus in boiling water for 1 minute. Then plunge into ice-cold water. When they're cold, cut each spear in half.

Carefully break the leaves away from the core of the little gems and wash, draining well. Cut the tomatoes in half and put them on an oven tray, drizzle with a little olive oil, sprinkle over the garlic, rosemary, thyme and sea salt and cook in a preheated oven at 80ºC/170ºF/gas mark 3 for 2 to 3 hours, checking occasionally.

Put the cornflour, flour, ginger, fourspice and coriander in a bowl and whisk in some ice-cold sparkling water, until you have a batter which coats the spoon.

Put all the salad ingredients into a large bowl – the potatoes, black olives, asparagus, little gem and tomatoes – and pour over some balsamic dressing. Toss and divide on to four plates. Pan-fry the ceps until golden and tender, then put to one side. Dip the prawns into the batter and put into a deep-fat fryer at 180ºC and fry until golden brown (if you don't have a deep-fat fryer put some oil in an ordinary pan and heat until very hot – but do be careful and do not leave unattended). Drain the prawns on kitchen paper and sprinkle with salt. Add the ceps to the salad then put the prawns on top. Eat immediately.

Crispy Sesame Prawns Served with a Pistou Salad

ingredients

Serves 4

1 red onion, sliced into thin rings
12 small new potatoes, cooked
60g French beans, cooked
4 baby artichokes, cooked
    and halved
4 spring onions, thinly sliced
4 plum tomatoes, peeled,
    deseeded and quartered
50g black olives
110g fresh, shaved Parmesan
a few mixed salad leaves
50g toasted croutons
50g pine nuts
50ml vinaigrette
16 tiger prawns
30g flour
30g cornflour
sparkling water
20g sesame seeds

Slice the new potatoes while they are still warm and sprinkle with a little lemon juice. Place them in the centre of the plate, along with the halved artichokes. (You can prepare the artichokes yourself or buy them from your delicatessen already marinated.)

Arrange the onion rings on top of the potatoes and artichokes, and then sprinkle with the croutons and olives. Place the tomatoes around the edge of the potatoes. Top all of this with the lightly dressed salad leaves.

Make the batter by mixing together the flour and the cornflour. Add the sesame seeds and then combine the sparkling water. Dip the prawns in the batter to coat them and deep fry at 180ºC until golden and crisp. Season with a little salt and arrange on the plate.

Finally, top the salad with the fresh Parmesan shavings.

the oyster seekers

Prawn, Samphire and Seabeet Tart

ingredients

Serves 4

1 batch shortcrust pastry
   (see page 194)
200g seabeet
100g samphire
16 tiger prawns, peeled
25g pine nuts
50g sun-blushed tomatoes
½ pint cream
¼ pint milk
¼ pint crème fraiche
2 whole eggs, plus one egg yolk
tartlet cases, 4½ inches wide
   by ¼ inch deep

Line the tartlet cases with the rested pastry (see page 194) and bake blind at 180°C. Once the cases are cooked and have cooled down, remove the baking beans and greaseproof paper.

Pick through the seabeet and then blanch in salted water for one minute. Refresh in cold water immediately and, when cold, lightly squeeze out any excess water.

Lightly toast the pine nuts until golden. Mix together in a bowl the cream, milk, crème fraiche and eggs. Lightly blanch the prawns in salted water, then remove and refresh in cold water. As soon as they are cold, pat them dry on kitchen paper.

Distribute the seabeet between the tartlets, along with the samphire, sun-blushed tomatoes and prawns. Pour the cream mixture over and top with pine nuts. Place in a pre-heated oven and cook at 190°C until set and golden. Serve with a green salad.

the oyster seekers

CHAPTER 4

Lobster and Crab

lobster

Lobsters really are the kings of crustaceans with their noble appearance and abundance of sweet and meaty succulent flesh – not to mention all the fun of crushing the claws to get out the tastiest morsels.

Delia remembers, when she was a child, the man who used to take to a rowing boat between the two piers of Herne Bay and Hampton, catch lobsters with a drop net and come up with dozens of them. Usually, of course, they are caught in baited lobster pots. They are partial to just about everything: shrimps, prawns, cockles, clams, oysters if they can get their claws in. Basically anything that moves. Sometimes, if you're very lucky and there's an exceptionally low tide, you might even walk out on the flats and find one; if the tide leaves them behind they'll bury themselves until the sea returns.

'Once, when I was child, there was a wreck of a sailing boat which suddenly opened up after a very low tide,' says Delia. 'The adults had put on big thigh boots and walked for ages to look at the wreck. She'd really opened up and inside there were literally dozens, if not hundreds, of lobsters – it was an amazing sight. I just stood there watching, covered in mud. The lobsters, of course, didn't last long. The grown-ups were soon there and the lobsters were soon gone – into the kitchen.'

These days in Whitstable, the lobsters make their way to the lobster pots and surrender to the table from May to November. Come the following Easter, the fishermen keep their eyes alert again. Lobsters don't like water that's too cold or too rough, and they can move fast. Their legs are in the front under their heads but, like prawns, they have swimerettes – the pointy bit under their tails. They use the legs and swimerettes to go forwards, but if they sense danger they can flip their tails as well, go forwards or backwards and, at the first sign of prey, they're off.

Lobsters are quite old when we eat them. In their first weeks of life they're very small – even smaller than shrimps – and shed their shells again and again, each one becoming tougher than the last. They are ingenious creatures. Each time they lose that early baby shell they crawl out and grow another, pumping up the new one with water until it's a third bigger than they are. Then they find somewhere to hide for a couple of weeks while they grow, maybe a large rock with space beneath, and the new shell hardens off. Each time if they survive, they become less and less vulnerable to being eaten by other fish – who, like us, have always found lobsters

COOKING AND PREPARING LOBSTER

The traditional way to cook a live lobster is to put it straight into boiling water but you might find your guilty conscience spoils your appetite – a little. The RSPCA say that the most humane way to kill the lobster is to put it in a plastic bag and then freeze it for two hours first. This stuns the lobster and it is unconscious when it goes into the boiling water.

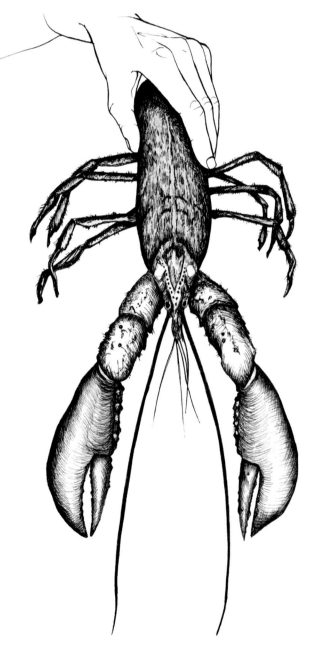

to be a most delicious lunch. Even then, the young lobster's shell isn't as hard as we are used to seeing in the fishmonger and, apart from watching out for other fish, the lobster has to keep one of its beady eyes out for other lobsters. They are carnivorous and there's nothing a big lobster likes more for tea than a little lobster – even if they are related.

When it reaches the table the very smallest lobster will be two or three years old. If stretched out it should be about 8 inches long and usually weighs about half a kilo. That makes a good lunch for one person. But, of course, you can never tell. In the restaurant, according to Delia, they've had enormous lobsters that weighed a stone or so and it's all been shell. These are old boys that have lived a long time and managed to keep growing their shells for protection. At other times, big lobsters fulfil all hopes and they're full of meat. Once, in the shop, they had one of 14lbs – one of the claws alone weighed 6lbs. It was meaty and delicious, and sold to one lucky Wheelerite for a spectacular dinner party.

But, basically, if you're shopping for lobster, work on the idea that one of a pound or so – or half a kilo – is good for one person; one of a pound and three-quarters – or three-quarters of a kilo – cooked and split in half will feed two. You'll notice that the two claws are not of the same size. This is because they serve different purposes for the lobster: one claw is the holder, he holds his prey with that; the other, with the serrated edge, is the cutter which enables

the oyster seekers

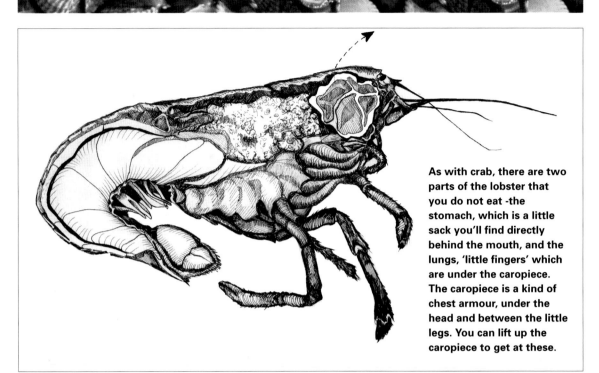

As with crab, there are two parts of the lobster that you do not eat - the stomach, which is a little sack you'll find directly behind the mouth, and the lungs, 'little fingers' which are under the caropiece. The caropiece is a kind of chest armour, under the head and between the little legs. You can lift up the caropiece to get at these.

the lobster to get to the meat of the prey. From our point of view the holder is the fatter and usually the juiciest.

Like everyone else in the fish business Delia has a great respect for lobsters and treats them with care. 'If you're going to pick up a lobster always hold it behind the head – never by the tail,' she says. 'It will flap like mad and that's when people drop them because they're scared. That's of no use at all. It hurts the lobster and damages them for cooking. I remember when I was young and my mother forgot once. We had a big beech table covered by enamel in our kitchen and she got badly cut by the lobster's cutting claw. She was extremely annoyed – with herself.

'Occasionally we get people in the shop who want to play around with the live lobsters that have just come in – usually men. It's a very silly thing to do but men seem to have a thing about prodding lobsters. If they met one while swimming in the sea they wouldn't be quite so brave. One customer started prodding a big live lobster with the wooden stave of a broom. The lobster didn't like it and broke the broom handle with ease. That man didn't ever play with lobsters again.'

One of the greatest fears people have about cooking live lobsters is that they will scream as they die in the boiling water, and the RSPCA recommend they should be put into the freezer for a while before boiling which will stun them. But Delia says: 'I've cooked hundreds of lobsters in boiling water and I've never heard one scream yet – you hear the blub, blub, blub

Once these are removed, slice the lobster completely in half and remove the black intestinal strip that runs along its back. The orange roe and the green liver, or tomalley, are both edible and delicious. Pull the claws back and snap off then, crack them with a hammer. The lobster is then ready to eat cold or for cooking. The meat from the claws can be removed with a lobster pick.

of air escaping from the shells – but they don't scream.'

If you have the nerve to cook your own live lobster you need to plunge it into boiling salted water, bring it back to the boil and then simmer for 12 to 15 minutes maximum, for a half-kilo lobster. As the weight increases, cook for another 3 minutes per half-kilo.

Once cooked you can prepare the lobster. As with crab, you don't eat the stomach – which is a little sack directly behind the mouth – or the lungs, which you find under the caropiece (a piece of chest armour under the head between the claws and the little legs).

Once you've removed these, slice the lobster completely in half, take out the black intestinal strip that runs along the back and that's more or less it, apart from hammering the hard claws with something like the back of an oyster knife so it's easy to get the flesh out. The green liver, or tomalley, is considered to be a delicacy and delicious on toast; the orange roe is also tasty but too hard to spread on toast, so eat as you go. Sometimes you will find black roe, which is basically unformed roe. This is sometimes known as lobster caviar and is also gorgeous on toast.

As for the rest of the lobster, eat the succulent meat with a good mayonnaise and salad on the side and some new potatoes or crusty bread. Or simply smother the halves in garlic butter and grill briefly until the butter is melted. There are endless ways to cook a lobster and most are mouthwatering – included here are some that are used in the restaurant.

the oyster seekers

Lobsters Poached in an Aromatic Court Bouillon

ingredients

Serves 4

1 portion of court bouillon
    (see recipe page 187)
4 fresh live lobsters of about
    500g each, preferably local but
    Canadian will do
clarified butter and a few chopped
    chives and chervil to serve

Bring the court bouillon to the boil. Cook the lobsters for about 8 to 10 minutes in the court bouillon. Remove when cooked and, using a cloth and being very careful not to burn your hands, prepare the lobster according the diagrams on pages 82 and 83.

Crack the claws with some lobster crackers if you have them (a good investment if you really love lobster), if not use a hammer. Then remove as much meat as you can from the claws using a lobster pick (an equally good investment).

Brush the halves of lobster with a little clarified butter and sprinkle over the chopped chives and chervil. Serve immediately with the cracked claws, a crisp green salad and some buttered new potatoes.

Lobster Thermidor

ingredients

Serves 4

2 live lobsters of about 675g each
2 tbsp hollandaise
   (see recipe page 193)
300ml bechamel sauce
   (see recipe page 191)
100g butter
2 shallots, finely diced
100ml dry white wine
50ml double cream
2 tsp Dijon mustard
2 tsp grated Parmesan cheese
25ml brandy
150ml fish stock

Place the lobsters in the freezer for an hour. This will not kill them but will make them sleepy. Then place each lobster on a board. Hold the tail end down firmly, take a sharp knife and firmly push it through the nerve centre of the head (this is marked by a cross at the back of the head) cutting all the way through the head. Now turn the lobster around and cut through the tail producing a split lobster. Remove the little sack from the head and the intestine trail. Pull off two large claws, right back to the head of the lobster – that's where a lot of the meat is – and blanch in boiling salted water for 1 minute then refresh in cold water. Remove immediately, crack open and leave to one side.

Melt half the butter in a pan and add the shallots, allowing them to sweat for 4 minutes ensuring that they do not brown. Add the brandy and flambé. When the flames die down, add all the lobsters, cover with a lid and leave to cook very slowly for 2–3 minutes. The shell should now be bright pink and the flesh opaque. Take the lobsters out of the pan and put on a baking tray, place the claws and lobster knuckles in the head of the lobster.

Add the wine to the shallots and brandy and reduce down to virtually nothing. Add the stock and reduce by half. Then add enough bechamel sauce to the stock to make a sauce of coating consistency. Whisk the cream and mustard into the sauce, bring back to the boil, check the seasoning and the consistency. Allow to cool for a minute, then fold in the hollandaise. Spoon the sauce over the lobsters in their shells so the meat is evenly covered. Dust lightly with Parmesan and glaze under a hot grill for a minute or two. Serve immediately.

the oyster seekers

Lobsters Grilled with Garlic Butter

ingredients

Serves 4

4 live lobsters of about 500g each
225g unsalted butter at room
    temperature
1 tbsp chopped parsley
1 lemon
2 cloves of garlic, crushed
    and puréed
salt and cayenne

Blanch the lobsters in boiling, well-salted water for two minutes. Remove and immediately place in ice-cold water. When the lobsters are cold, remove from the water – make sure you leave them in there for as short a time as possible, as they are like sponges and soak up water.

Mix the butter with a good squeeze of lemon juice, a pinch of cayenne, the garlic, the chopped parsley and some salt to season. Split the lobsters in half and remove the black intestinal trail along with the mouthpiece. Evenly distribute the butter over the lobsters and place under a hot grill for 5 minutes.

Serve with a nice crisp green salad and crusty bread or glazed vegetables and new potatoes.

Lobster Bisque

If you're cooking lobsters for a meal, save the heads and you can use them in a lobster bisque. If not, get them from your fishmonger.

ingredients

Serves 4

900g lobster heads (remove
the small legs as they can
burn quite easily)
olive oil
butter
1 carrot, roughly diced
1 large onion, roughly diced
2 celery sticks, chopped
1 bulb fennel, chopped
1 clove garlic, chopped
200ml white wine
100ml Armagnac
1 tbsp tomato purée
3 ripe tomatoes, chopped
lemon juice, cayenne, salt
and pepper
1.5–2 litres of fish stock (see
recipe page 188)
a bay leaf and sprig of thyme
a few tarragon leaves
200ml double cream

Crush the lobster heads with a rolling pin. Melt the butter in a large pan, then add the carrot, onion, celery, fennel, garlic and bay leaf, and allow to sweat for 10 minutes, with no colour, until the veg is nice and soft. Add the chopped tomatoes, tomato purée and a pinch of cayenne pepper, and allow to cook for another 5 minutes. Add the crushed lobster heads and shells, then the Armagnac – flambé if you can – then add the white wine and carry on cooking until the mixture is reduced by about a third.

Bring the fish stock to the boil in another pan, then add to your lobster mix so that the shells are completely covered. Add the lemon juice, thyme and tarragon, and simmer for 40 minutes. Blend the mixture, including half of the shells, in a food processor, then pass through a fine sieve. Put the mixture in a clean pan and add any extra fish stock you haven't used to alter the consistency if needed. Add a good squeeze of lemon juice and the cream, and check your seasoning.

To serve, put a drop of Armagnac in each bowl, give the soup a little whisk so it's a little frothy, then pour on to the Armagnac in the bowls. You can add some warmed lobster meat if you have any and finish off with a pinch of cayenne pepper. Needless to say this rich soup is virtually a meal on its own.

Lobster Caesar Salad

ingredients

Serves 4

2 cos lettuces
4 x 500g lobsters
2 lemons, cut into segments
100g sun-dried tomatoes
100g croutons
100g fresh Parmesan
Caesar dressing
150g Jersey Royals
16 fresh anchovies
26g sesame seeds
50g cornflour
sparkling water
4 litres court bouillon
   (see page 187)
100g clarified butter

FOR THE CAESAR DRESSING:
1 egg yolk
30g grated Parmesan
juice of ¼ lemon
splash of cider vinegar
100ml groundnut oil
a dash of hot water (if needed)

Bring the court bouillon to the boil in a large pan. Place the lobsters in the liquid, and bring back to a simmer. Remove from the heat and allow to go cold. Lightly wash the potatoes and cook in plenty of boiling water. Once cooked, remove from the water. Place in a bowl and drizzle with some vinaigrette and chopped chives.

Place the croutons into a hot pan with some clarified butter. Cook until they are golden brown and crispy. Drain on kitchen paper and allow to go cold.

Remove the lobsters from the court bouillon. Remove their claws and knuckles and then remove the shell, keeping the meat intact. Split the lobster in half and remove the tail meat.

To make the Caesar dressing, place the egg yolk, Parmesan, garlic, anchovies, cider vinegar and lemon juice into a hand blender and blitz thoroughly. Add the groundnut oil until you have achieved the taste you want and the dressing has emulsified. If the dressing thickens too much, just let it down with a little warm water.

Remove the outer leaves of the lettuce, ensuring that they are kept whole. Wash and dry them, removing any dirt, then divide them amongst the plates. Cut the rest of the lettuce into good bite-size pieces. Dress with a little Caesar dressing and add to the other leaves.

Divide the lemon segments, tomatoes, croutons and lobster among the plates. Finish with a few fresh shavings of Parmesan. To top the dish, blend both flours together with the sesame seeds. Add a little sparkling water to create a light batter. Dip the anchovies in the batter, and deep fry at 170ºC, until crispy. Add to the prepared plates along with the rewarmed Jersey Royals.

Lobster Recipes from Another Age

The Victorians, like medieval cooks, were very keen on aspic and jellies. They loved their shellfish and crustaceans too. This elaborate recipe by Mrs A. B. Marshall was called Lobster Mayonnaise à l'Osborne (Mayonnaise de Homard à l'Osborne). Osborne, on the Isle of Wight, was a favourite family home of Queen Victoria and Prince Albert and, as this recipe appears in a book of 1895, it's safe to assume that the royal family tucked into this dish occasionally. It would certainly have kept the cook busy. She would have been expected to be as much of an artist as a chef – decoration, as well as taste, was all-important and food, at least for some, was expected to look pretty.

Cut from cucumber, by means of a pea cutter, some pea-shaped pieces, and cook these till tender by putting them in cold water with a little salt and boiling them; also cut out some similar pieces of hard-boiled white of egg and cooked beetroot. Line some little bouche cups thinly with aspic jelly, and garnish them in rings with the pea shapes of cucumber, egg, beetroot and also French capers, arranging these ingredients alternately on the aspic that the colours may have a pretty effect, and covering the bottom of the moulds and halfway up the sides with these rings, garnish round the rest of the sides with little picked leaves of chervil, and set the garnish with a little more aspic.

Remove the shell from a freshly cooked lobster, and cut the back piece of the fish in round slices about a quarter of an inch thick, place one in each of the prepared moulds, and fill the moulds up with mayonnaise aspic, and put them aside to set. Line, garnish and prepare a fluted border mould in the same manner, fill it up with picked shrimps, and set them similarly with aspic mayonnaise, and let it set. When ready to dish up, dip the border mould in warm water, pass a cloth over the bottom to absorb any moisture, and turn the border out onto an entrée dish, and place a prepared wax figure in the centre of the border [these were something like the decorations we use on cakes today but made of wax]*; turn out the little bouche cups in a similar manner, placing one on each of the flutes of the border and one on top of the wax figure; fill up round the centre of the figure with a mixture of the pea-shaped vegetables, having first seasoned them with a little salad oil and tarragon vinegar, and mixed in a little picked tarragon and chervil; arrange a little also round the top of the waxed figure. Place in the hollow of each little bouche shapes a little mayonnaise, and garnish this mayonnaise alternately with sprigs of tarragon, chervil and coralline pepper. Garnish the dish with chopped aspic and little bunches of the seasoned pea-shaped vegetables.*

Mrs A. B. Marshall wasn't just a shrewd woman – she was an industry. In the nineteenth century she wrote and sold tens of thousands of cookbooks and she ran a famous cookery school, Marshall's School of Cookery, in London's West End. But that was just part of her empire. She also manufactured and sold just about everything a cook could possibly need in the kitchen – she'd even design and furnish the entire kitchen for you. She sold baking powder and jelly bags, concentrated essences, fruit syrups, peppers, curry powder, tinned sardines and rum – they all carried her name. Then there were the saucepans (from 2 shillings 4 pence to 12 shillings each), ladles, knives, bowls and moulds of all shapes and sizes from butterflies to swans. She was also successful selling a very nifty gadget called 'Marshall's Patent Ice Cave'. It was a metal 'safe' with an inner box – the 'cave'. If you filled the gap between the two with ice it kept the food cold, if filled with hot water it kept dishes hot.

Somehow she also managed to travel the country giving lectures and demon-strations. She was very popular. In fact, she was a star. As the *Newcastle Chronicle* wrote in August, 1887:

We looked with a feeling of awe at the graceful kindly lady, who is rapidly raising cooking to a fine art. The most fastidious could watch Mrs Marshall with pleasure and the highest compliment that I can pay her is to say that after seeing her cook one longs to partake of the viands she has prepared.

crabs

Unlike lobsters, crabs can be vicious and bad-tempered. Lobsters at sea rarely fight each other (even though the big ones aren't averse to eating the little ones on occasion), but crabs at sea or on shore often get into a fight. Sometimes you can even hear them trying to tear each other's plates (shells) off. When you come across a dead crab on the beach with one of its claws torn off, the chances are it has been in a fight with another crab – and lost.

As with lobsters, you should always be careful when handling a live crab. Always hold it behind the head so its claws can't get at you. They may look ungainly wandering up the beach but once in the sea they're fast movers, using their tail as a rudder. They also have the advantage of having eyes on stalks, which can go up and down, and also see over their back. Like lobsters they also shed their shells regularly. It's like someone with tight shoes or a skirt that's too small – as they get fatter they need a bigger size.

Around here, most of the local crabs are caught in pots off Whitstable, Herne Bay and towards Broadstairs. Male and female crabs are easily distinguishable. The 'hens' are beamier (i.e. wider on the beam), they're full of coral and their flesh is very sweet. The 'cock' crabs have bigger claws – all the better to fight you with – but the flesh inside may not be so good.

The brown meat you find in a crab is the liver, and if it is quite orangey or has orangey flecks in it then you've hit on a hen crab and that's the roe. To cook a crab, you first put it into cold water and leave it for about 30 minutes. Then put it over a very low heat. Once the legs appear to have gone floppy, turn up the heat and bring to the boil. Boiling times are about 10 to 12 minutes for a medium crab of about half a kilo, increasing the cooking time by 5 minutes per half-kilo. The smallest crabs sold in the shop are about 5 inches across the canopy and weigh around half a kilo. But, of course, they come in all shapes and sizes. Delia remembers crabs from Devon which have measured about 13 inches across. When she was a child many fishermen used to paint sea scenes and oyster yawls inside dried, empty crab shells.

Many people are worried about the 'poisonous' dead men's fingers in a crab. These are the greeny lungs found behind the head. Before refrigeration, some fishmongers would cook the crabs, leave them whole and uncleaned on a marble slab to display them and then sprinkle them with crushed ice. And there they would stay for

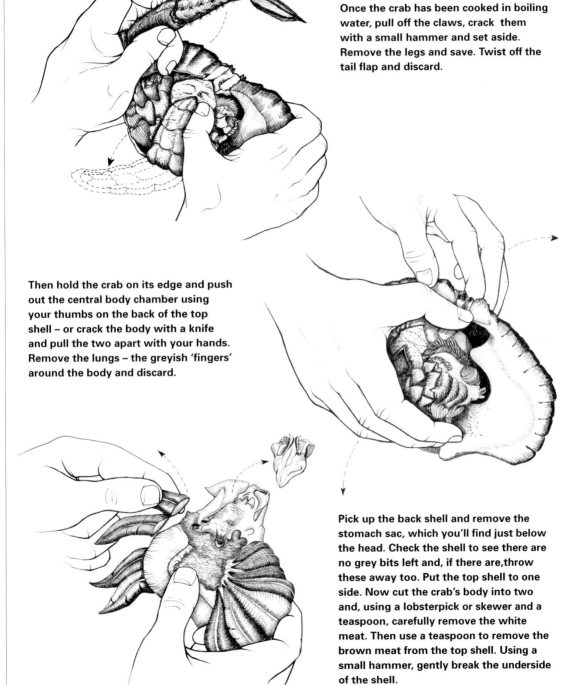

COOKING AND PREPARING A CRAB

Once the crab has been cooked in boiling water, pull off the claws, crack them with a small hammer and set aside. Remove the legs and save. Twist off the tail flap and discard.

Then hold the crab on its edge and push out the central body chamber using your thumbs on the back of the top shell – or crack the body with a knife and pull the two apart with your hands. Remove the lungs – the greyish 'fingers' around the body and discard.

Pick up the back shell and remove the stomach sac, which you'll find just below the head. Check the shell to see there are no grey bits left and, if there are, throw these away too. Put the top shell to one side. Now cut the crab's body into two and, using a lobsterpick or skewer and a teaspoon, carefully remove the white meat. Then use a teaspoon to remove the brown meat from the top shell. Using a small hammer, gently break the underside of the shell.

the day, looking very pretty. But all that water was seeping into the crabs and, with the warmth, the flesh was going slowly but surely rotten. These days you could eat a whole crab, lungs and all, and you'd be fine, although it wouldn't taste very nice.

Lobster is still more expensive in restaurants than crab but a good crab can be just as delicious. A whole prepared crab, maybe still slightly warm, with a good plain mayonnaise and perhaps a little salad is hard to beat. The brown meat of a crab on toast – with maybe a little white pepper and a tiny squidge of lemon juice – is very good, and a mixed brown and white meat crab sandwich, perhaps with a little cucumber, is an absolute winner.

Crayfish can be prepared as lobster although they are considerably smaller and have no meaty cutting claws. Instead, the feelers on their head, are much bigger, with two little holding hands underneath, and they have lumpy, bumpy shells. The sea isn't salty enough for crayfish immediately off the Kent coast – which is a shame – but, then, if the water were more salty we wouldn't get the oysters.

Pan-Fried Crab Cakes with Rocket, Apple and Walnut Salad

This is one of the most popular dishes on our menu and many people buy the cakes ready prepared to cook at home.

ingredients

Serves 4

450g fresh white crabmeat
1 bunch spring onions, cleaned, split lengthways, then finely diced
3 tbsp mayonnaise
10 drops Tabasco, i.e. a good splash
juice of half a lemon
225g fresh white breadcrumbs
2 bunches of rocket
3oz walnuts
1 apple
lemon wedges, salt and pepper

Check the crabmeat for any bits of shell, and keep covered in the fridge. Mix the mayonnaise with the spring onion, then add the Tabasco, lemon, salt and pepper. Mix well. Add the crabmeat and mix well again. Add only enough breadcrumbs to bind the mixture. Check the taste and consistency – it should just hold together in your hand. Weigh out into four portions and shape your crab cakes. Coat in more breadcrumbs, then put them, covered, in the fridge to set for between 12 and 24 hours.

To cook, pan-fry in a little oil until golden brown on one side, then turn over and place in the centre of a warm oven for 6 to 8 minutes. Pick over the rocket and dress with a vinaigrette. Add the roughly chopped walnuts and sliced apple.

Place salad on one side of the plate, leaving room for a nice, fat crabcake on the other. Serve with lemon wedges.

Crab Salad Finished with Avocado, Lime and Roasted Langoustine

ingredients

Serves 4

450g freshly picked white
  crabmeat
1 bunch of chives, chopped
half a red onion, finely chopped
1 avocado
1 dessertspoon sour cream
2 dessertspoon good mayonnaise
1 dessertspoon crème fraiche
a few salad leaves
juice of half a lemon
1 cos lettuce
1 tsp caviar
12 live langoustines
2 tsp vinaigrette
1 lime
1 red chilli

Pick through the fresh white crabmeat, removing any bits of shell. Cover and keep in the fridge. Blanch the live langoustine for 1 minute in boiling salted water. Remove immediately and place in ice-cold water. Remove the heads from the langoustines (keep them for stock or soup later on), and carefully peel off the shells removing the black intestinal trail where possible. Put in a bowl, cover and allow to rest in the fridge.

Mix the mayonnaise with a good squeeze of lemon juice, the chopped chives and red onion, and season with salt and pepper. Fold the white crabmeat into the mixture.

Shred the lettuce and mix with a little crème fraiche. Peel the avocado and blend in a food processor with the lime juice and some more salt and pepper. Finely dice the chilli and mix this in with the avocado.

To make the caviar dressing: take a dessertspoon of sour cream, season with a little salt and pepper and lightly fold in the caviar (do this gently or you'll end up with a grey mass).

To serve: take a round mould about 6cm wide and 3cm high. Put the mould in the centre of the plate. Put a little of the lettuce and crème fraiche mixture at the bottom of the mould, then spoon in the crab mixture until the mould is three-quarters full. Top up with the avocado mixture. Now roast the langoustines in a little oil until golden and cooked – for how long depends on the size of the langoustines, but it shouldn't take very long. Judge when cooked by the colour and firmness of the shellfish. Divide the langoustines among four plates. Put a little of the caviar dressing around the plate, dress the salad leaves, remove the moulds from the crab mixture. Place the salad leaves on top and serve immediately.

If you don't have small moulds there's a very good and cheap alternative for cold foods like the crab here – for example, plastic drainpipe. Simply ask your hardware store to cut you off some circles of plastic drainpipe to the depth you want.

Crab Tabbouleh

ingredients

Serves 4

225g couscous (you can use bulgar wheat as an alternative)

2 tomatoes, peeled, deseeded and diced

half a cucumber, deseeded and diced

1 medium red onion, finely diced

1 bunch of flat leaf parsley, chopped

350ml boiling water

225g fresh white crabmeat

20 leaves fresh mint, chopped carefully, so as not to bruise the leaves

a good squeeze of lemon juice

olive oil, sea salt to season

Put the couscous in a bowl, add the boiling water, sprinkle over a little sea salt to season and add a little olive oil. Cover with clingfilm and leave for about 45 minutes. Then mix the mint and parsley into the couscous, together with the onion, tomato and cucumber. Lightly fold in the crabmeat, add a good squeeze of lemon juice and check the seasoning. Serve in a big bowl, sprinkle with more parsley and serve with warm pitta bread.

the oyster seekers

Crab, Sweetcorn and Spring Onion Risotto

ingredients

Serves 4

2 tsp mascarpone cheese
250g risotto rice
3 corn on the cob, fresh
4 spring onions
250g white crabmeat
100ml white wine
600ml vegetable or chicken stock
1 white onion, finely diced
butter
30g grated Parmesan
2 tsp chopped chives
olive oil

Grate the corn kernels of two of the cobs with a grater, reserving the cobs for the stock. Melt a good knob of butter in a pan, add the grated corn and, on a low heat, allow to cook out until all the moisture has evaporated. Place this corn mixture in a food processor and blend to a fine purée. Put the other cob into a pan of boiling water and cook for 4–5 minutes. When the kernels are tender, remove from the pan and refresh the cob in cold water. Take a sharp knife and cut away the kernels from the cob, reserving the cob. Put the bare corn cobs into the chicken stock, bring to the boil and allow to simmer for 45 minutes.

Warm a little olive oil, add the onion and cook gently for a couple of minutes, ensuring that the onion does not brown. Add the rice and continue cooking for another couple of minutes. Add the wine and allow to reduce to virtually nothing. Add the stock, ladle by ladle, stirring all the time. Continue this process until the risotto is cooked, which will take about 8–10 minutes.

Now stir in the sweetcorn purée and the sweetcorn kernels, and, in this order, add the spring onions, crabmeat and chives – still stirring. Fold in the mascarpone cheese and Parmesan. Taste, adjust the seasoning and serve immediately.

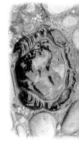

the oyster seekers

Crab Recipes from Another Age

crabe diable
(devilled crab)

Lightly fry in butter some chopped onion and shallot. Remove and swill the pan with a few drops of brandy, adding then a little Dijon mustard, a little bechamel sauce and the flesh of a crab. Season according to taste and garnish the crab shells with this mixture.

*MADAME PRUNIER'S FISH COOKERY
BOOK, REVISED (1959)*

This is a classic recipe from the famous Madame Prunier. A Frenchwoman and daughter of leading fishery expert and restaurateur Emile Prunier. Madame Prunier was a wonderful cook who ran restaurants in London and Paris in the 1930s, 40s and 50s. She specialised in fish cookery and created dishes from the simple and delicious, like the one above, to the extravagant – and delicious – cordon bleu. As author Ambrose Heath wrote in the Fifties:

It is an odd thing that to an island race, used perhaps to eating fish more than most other European nations, a Frenchwoman should have come to teach us how to prepare it but perhaps not so odd after all, since it was a woman bearing a name which is a household word in Europe for fish. Madame Prunier opened her restaurant in London, and she hit the spirit of the time, by beginning to popularise the cheaper sorts of fish, herring, mackerel, gurnard, skate – fishes which we had been used to look at askance. And she accomplished what was almost a miracle by inducing fashionable diners-out to ask for herrings – and to like them too.

the oyster seekers

CHAPTER 5

Winkles, Whelks and Eels

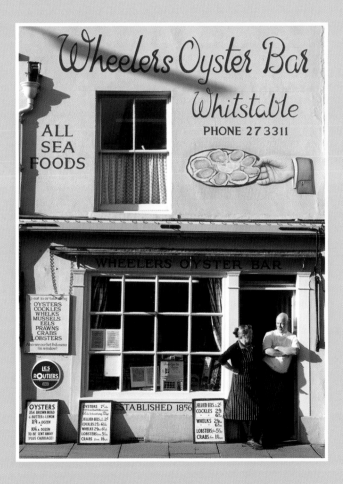

winkles

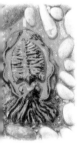

Winkles are a lovely little shellfish. They're fiddly and it's time-consuming to get them out of their browny-black shells with a toothpick (or preferably an Edwardian hatpin!) but they are worth the effort, and the process of picking out and eating them can be very therapeutic. There are many less pleasurable ways of spending an hour or so.

Winkles are plentiful all around the coast and it's easy to pick your own. You'll find them on the beach, on the groynes or just about anywhere, but again be careful if you find them attached to anything iron. These won't do you any good at all, so give them a miss. Also, be warned that if you want to pick your own you are letting yourself in for some hard work.

Watch out for the chitters (barnacles) and choose winkles that are chitter-free, merely to cut your labour in half: chitters are likely to be full of mud and they're hard to remove. Once picked, you need to put the winkles into lots of salt water and wash them thoroughly. Then place them in more salt water, give them another wash, and then possibly even a third. Remove the winkles with a wire basket and see how much mud you have left in the water. Keep washing until there's next to no mud left at the bottom. There is nothing worse than a gritty winkle. Usually you will need three washes, at least three minutes each. Remember to use lots of cooking salt.

When you're finally satisfied that they're cleaned as much as possible put the winkles in boiling water for 12 minutes. Remove them, put into cold salted water to cool down, shake in a colander to get rid of the excess water and then they are ready.

Winkles are exceptionally delicious served with Worcestershire sauce as a dip, and brown bread and butter. They can also be cooked in a variety of recipes (if you've got the patience – and many people love them so much that they have) or they make good decorative extras to many seafood dishes such as pasta.

You can pick winkles all year round, but here in the south, we sell them only in the winter. The winkle likes a good browse on summer seaweed and everybody knows what seaweed smells like in summer. Eating them during this time of year won't harm you, but they do taste a little strong. Winter winkles are best.

Baked Winkles with a Garlic and Herb Butter Served on Warm Toast

ingredients

Serves 2

1 pint freshly picked
   cooked winkles
50g garlic butter
2 slices brown toast
lemon wedges

Place the winkles on an oven tray. Evenly distribute the garlic butter over the winkles and place into a pre-heated oven at 190°C/375°F/gas mark 5. Allow the butter to melt over the winkles, stir occasionally or give them a bit of a shake – but don't burn your hands. Toast the bread on both sides. Put on individual plates, top with winkles and spoon over the melted garlic butter. Serve with a large wedge of lemon – and winkle picks, needles or toothpicks for removing the hot winkles.

the oyster seekers

A Sunday Tea of Winkles

ingredients

Serves 4

2 pints winkles, freshly cooked
8 slices of brown bread
2 bunches of watercress
malt vinegar for dipping
4 lemon wedges
2 tbsp vinaigrette

Butter the bread, remove the crusts and cut in half on the diagonal. Pick over the watercress, discarding any tough stalks and toss in a little vinaigrette. Serve the winkles, watercress and bread and butter on individual plates with a bowl of malt vinegar for dipping. And don't forget, of course, a good pot of tea.

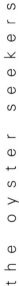

the oyster seekers

whelks

You either love them or loathe them. Whelks are an acquired taste. Many people love them straight with vinegar but others say they taste like old rubber. That's not fair on the whelk. They should never be overcooked or they easily toughen up. The Japanese adore whelks – many from Whitstable have been frozen and made their way to Japan where they are defrosted, then removed from their shells and used in stir-fries and broths.

Delia likes her whelks neat and still warm from the copper – no vinegar. Like sugar spoils tea, she says, vinegar spoils the whelk. Mark uses them as a strong flavour in soups and in the recipes we've included here. One elderly lady customer who has adored whelks for 60 years, developed a problem with her teeth – i.e. she lacked them – so she couldn't chew whelks any more, and they do need to be chewed, it's part of the pleasure. She adapted accordingly, put her whelks through the mincer and swears they come out just like crabmeat. These she spreads on toast, adding a little salt and pepper and a tiny drop of vinegar, and says they are delicious – like nothing else.

The whelks we get in Whitstable are all local, although they like cold and deep water and as our local coastal waters warm up there may be a few weeks of the year when the whelk refuses to show itself.

Before the whelk is bashed about by the tides on the beach – or cooked – it has a browny-coloured shell which almost feels like suede to the touch. They used to be fished for in whelk pots – a little like miniature lobster pots – or shanks, several pots on a rope. The pots had holes in the bottom and a net at the top so once the whelks crawled in they couldn't get out. In the middle of the pot hung a piece of rope and attached to the rope was a bait ring, which carried a bit of fish bait, the smellier the better. The whelks found it hard to resist and became trapped. These days they're usually caught in plastic drums, containing a lump of cement at the bottom to anchor them, but there is still a piece of rope across the top and some bait, like a piece of fish or crab.

Whitstable fishermen continue to go whelking, and find some of the best whelks in England. Derek West is one. He can be found selling his haul at the harbour.

Cooked Whelks

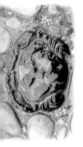

ingredients

1 gallon raw fresh whelks
2 gallons water
3 tbsp table salt
Malt vinegar and brown bread
   and butter to serve

Wash the whelks well to remove as much mud and grit etc. as possible. Put the water and salt in a pan. Allow to boil in small batches if you haven't a saucepan big enough for the lot. When boiling, add the whelks, putting a lid on top. Bring back to boil quickly. Remove lid. Turn down heat and allow to simmer for 12 to 15 minutes depending how big your whelks are. With a ladle, skim off any scum that comes to the surface. When cooked, drain through a colander and allow to cool. Either eat warm (Delia's favourite – neat) or leave until cold. Use a lobster pick or skewer to remove the whelks. First, remove the opercuccum (the plastic-looking disc at the mouth of the shell). Pierce the whelk and pull while turning the shell so the whelk comes out easily. (You can use the same technique with winkles.) Serve with malt vinegar, brown bread and butter.

You can alter the amount of whelks you use according to what you need, just adjust the proportions of the other ingredients accordingly.

Whelk, Squid, Basil and Pancetta Linguine

ingredients

Serves 4

375g linguine

400g cooked whelks, removed
from their shells

10 tubes of baby squid, cleaned
and cut in half

5 spring onions, sliced thinly

8 thin slices of pancetta

small bunch of basil, picked over,
cleaned and torn

2 cloves of garlic, crushed
into a purée

a pinch of chilli flakes

2 plum tomatoes, blanched,
peeled, deseeded and diced

juice of one lemon

a little olive oil

Slice the whelks very thinly with a sharp knife, discarding the tail. Put to one side. Cook the linguine in boiling salted water until tender. While the pasta is cooking, put the pancetta under the grill until crisp. Heat a pan with a little olive oil, season the squid and pan-fry very quickly once the oil is hot. Remove and keep warm. The squid will take no more than 1 or 2 minutes. Sweat the spring onions and garlic in another pan (big enough to add the rest of the ingredients). Add the drained linguine, squid, whelks, diced tomato and chilli flakes. Toss together over the heat and lightly fold in the basil leaves until it's all thoroughly mixed. Add a quick squeeze of lemon juice and olive oil. Divide between individual serving plates, top with the crispy pancetta and serve immediately.

eels

Look in just about any Victorian cookbook designed for the lady of the house and you're bound to find at least one recipe for eel: eel pies, eel soufflés, eel stews. These days the eel has gone out of fashion, although you might find it in some sophisticated London restaurants – where they consider themselves to be daring including it on the menu … and charge accordingly. Of course, pie and mash shops, where you can eat stewed eels with green liquor and lovely mash, are happily still with us, and jellied eels remain a stalwart of the seaside.

The trouble with the eel is that, in its raw state, it is hardly the most appetising of fish. It is ugly. And it wriggles. This, of course, is not the fault of the eel. Its good points are that it can taste delicious; it's meaty, nutritious, cheap (at the moment) and it's versatile – there are a hundred and one things you can do with an eel.

Eels are abundant off the coast of East Kent and are still caught here in large numbers – many of the jellied eels sold in London and beyond began life off the Whitstable shores. They're fast swimmers and called 'silver eels' locally because at certain times of the year their skins turn silver and you can see them skimming through the water like shafts of light. Then there are the conger eels – rarer but out there nevertheless. You really don't want to meet one of those. The silver eels are usually about two feet long when they're ready to be caught – the conger is three

times the size, has a big head, big jaws and razor sharp teeth that can easily bite your fingers off. Fortunately, you don't see many of them. They don't like us and we don't like them.

If you want to experiment with cooking eel you'd be wise to go to your local fishmonger, who will no doubt be delighted to see you (fishmongers appreciate eels and can't understand why everyone else doesn't). Preparing an eel yourself isn't an altogether pleasant experience – Delia remembers as a child watching her fisherman father gutting and cleaning a writhing eel in the kitchen sink. Since then she gets her eels fresh from Whitstable. Those which are not needed in the kitchen are then sent to 'the lads in London at Billingsgate' which then make their way back to Whitstable – dead and jellied.

As far as the restaurant is concerned it isn't worth the time or effort of making their

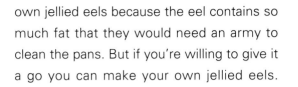

own jellied eels because the eel contains so much fat that they would need an army to clean the pans. But if you're willing to give it a go you can make your own jellied eels.

Just ensure you buy plenty of washing-up liquid because you will be washing up the fat for quite a time afterwards.

making jellied eels

Ask your fishmonger to gut and chop the eel but keep the skin on. Bring it to the boil in a saucepan of water which completely covers the pieces. Add allspice or peppercorns. Add some chopped onions, port or Madeira, bring back to the boil and cook for just another 3 minutes or so – you don't want to overcook the eel or it comes away from the bone. Take the eel pieces out of the liquor, strain the liquid to get rid of any bits, add a little more allspice if you like your jelly tangy, boil fast for about 5 to 10 minutes. Sieve the liquid again and cover the eel pieces. Leave to cool, then chill and you have wonderful jellied eels.

the oyster seekers

Eel Soufflé with Garlic and Parsley Served with Marinière Sauce

ingredients

Serves 10 –12

400g fresh eel, skinned, gutted
    and filleted
100g smoked eel
2 lots of 2 egg whites
6 whole garlic cloves
small bunch of flat-leafed parsley
1½ pints double cream
28g grated Parmesan cheese
a bag of ice (available from most
    off-licences)
salt, cayenne pepper
Marinière sauce (see recipe
    page 186)
a little goose fat

Firstly, smile at your fishmonger and ask him to prepare the eels for you. Cut the fresh eel and smoked eel into small pieces. Put both in a food processor and blend to a purée, then add two of the egg whites and continue blitzing until well blended. Pass the mixture through a fine sieve, put into a clean, grease-free bowl and put this bowl on ice, keeping the mixture as cold as possible. Season the eel mixture with a little salt and cayenne pepper. This will lightly firm up your mixture. Slowly fold in the cream a little at a time (the mixture may not take all the cream – or you might need a little more). What you want is a folding consistency, which means that when you pull the spatula out of the mixture it folds back on itself and doesn't sit there in a peak. Add some seasoning, cover the mixture with clingfilm and put in the fridge for 30 minutes.

Melt the goose fat over a high heat then turn down to a simmer. Add the peeled garlic cloves and simmer for 5–7 minutes. Turn off the heat, allow to cool, mash the garlic and pass through a sieve, then add to the eel mixture, mixing thoroughly. Make the Marinière sauce according to recipe. Grease the ramekins with a little butter and sprinkle in the Parmesan. Put in the fridge and chill for 10 minutes. Add the juice of one lemon to the eel mixture and put a third into a clean bowl.

Whisk the 2 remaining egg whites until they form soft peaks. Add a good pinch of salt and carry on whisking for a couple of minutes. Take a third of the whisked egg whites and beat into the eel mixture, then fold in the rest. Put into the ramekins and level the mixture off with a palette knife. Bake in a pre-heated oven at 190ºC for about 12 minutes, until the soufflés are just firm to the touch. Serve the ramekins on a plate with the rewarmed Marinière sauce. Rewarm the sauce and at the last moment add the shellfish.

Braised Eel with Lightly Spiced Rice

ingredients

Serves 4

3 medium eels, gutted
and cleaned
300g long grain rice
1 onion, finely diced
½ litre white wine
200ml fish stock
2 bay leaves
4 cloves
8 juniper berries
30g butter
3 tsp curry powder
1 tbsp fresh dill, chopped

Put the wine, stock, bay leaves, juniper berries and cloves into a pan. Bring to the boil and simmer for five minutes.

Cut the eels into inch-long pieces (or get your fishmonger to do this for you), add to the white wine mix and allow to simmer until the eels are tender. Remove the eels from the cooking liquor but spoon a little of the liquor over the eels to keep them moist.

Melt the butter in the pan, add the onion and cook gently for about 3 minutes with no colour. Add the rice and cook for another 2 minutes or so with no colour. Pour all the stock on to the rice adding the curry powder and all the spices from the stock. Bring back to the boil. Cover with buttered greaseproof paper. Put into a pre-heated oven at 230ºC/450ºF/gas mark 8, for 15 minutes.

Remove from the oven, put in a clean pan, add another a large knob of butter and lightly fork through along with the chopped dill. Remove the skin and bones from the eel – great fun – fold the meat into the mixture and serve immediately.

Smoked Eel with a Parsley Potato Cake and Poached Quails Eggs

ingredients

Serves 4

500g potatoes
1 bunch flat leaf parsley
100g baby spinach
4 quails eggs
100g mixed leaf salad
olive oil
4 x 100g pieces of smoked eel,
 skinned and off the bone
200g vine cherry tomatoes
150ml groundnut oil
salt and pepper
few sprigs of chervil

Peel and wash the potatoes. Place them in cold, salted water. Bring to the boil and allow to simmer until they are just tender. Drain the potatoes and allow them to dry out. Then pass them through a fine sieve. Add a small knob of butter and adjust seasoning to taste.

Pick all the parsley leaves from the parsley. Plunge them, along with the baby spinach, into a pan of boiling, salted water for about 1 minute. Remove immediately and place into a bowl of ice-cold water. When cold, remove from the water and squeeze thoroughly, to remove any excess water.

Place in a blender and blend until it is reduced to a fine purée. Moisten with a little oil if necessary. Pass the blended mixture through a fine sieve if you wish, or just leave it as it is before adding it to the potato mixture. It should turn your potato a vibrant green colour! Divide the potato into 4 and shape into rounds.

Place the tomatoes in a blender and blitz. Pass the pulp through a fine sieve, reserving the liquid. Return this to the cleaned blender, season, add the oil and blitz again to produce an extremely fresh tomato vinaigrette.

Pan fry the potato cakes on one side, until they are golden and crispy. Turn them over and warm them through in the oven for a few minutes. When cooked, remove them from the oven and place in the centre of each plate. Drizzle the tomato dressing around the plate. Dress the salad with some vinaigrette. Place the eel and then the dressed salad on top of the potato cake.

To finish the dish, carefully break the eggs into a bowl of cold water and vinegar and leave for a few minutes. Using a slotted spoon, place them into a pan of boiling water and cook for one minute. Remove and carefully place on the salad. Garnish the dish with a few sprigs of chervil.

Eel Stew

ingredients

Serves 4

3 medium eels, cleaned
    and gutted
25g flour
25g butter (at room temperature)
2 tbsp chopped parsley
400ml double cream
salt and cayenne pepper

Cut the eel into inch-long pieces – or get your fishmonger to do this for you. Put into a pan and add just enough cold water to cover. Season with salt and cayenne. Bring to the boil. Allow to simmer gently for 15 to 20 minutes until the eels are cooked and tender. In the same pan melt the butter and add the flour to make a roux. When it is a golden colour, add the eel liquor, slowly stirring all the time until it's completely mixed. Bring back to the boil, add the cream, and simmer the sauce until the floury taste has disappeared. Add the chopped parsley, adjust the seasoning and return the eels to the sauce to reheat through. Serve immediately with warm, crusty bread.

Eel Recipes from Another Age

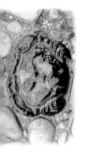

Eels were always traditionally served from big white enamel bowls. In the 1930s, when eels had taken over from oysters as the food of the less well-off, some eel men made a fortune. Robert Cooke, known as the Jellied Eel King, who had a pie and eel stall in Horseferry Road, London, before the Second World War, left £42,000 when he died – a fortune back then. Eels used to be spit-roasted or fried and served in a hot loaf. They were once plentiful in the Thames. Here are some old eel recipes:

eels in cream

Skin, empty [gut] and wash as clean as possible, two or three fine eels. Cut them into short lengths and just cover with cold water; add sufficient salt and cayenne to season them and stew them very softly [gently] from fifteen to twenty minutes or longer should they require it. When they are nearly done, strew over them a teaspoon of minced parsley, thicken the sauce with a spoonful of flour mixed with a slice of butter and add a quarter of a pint or more of clotted cream. Give the whole a boil, lift the fish into a hot dish and stir briskly the juice of half a lemon into the sauce; pour it upon the eels and serve immediately. Very thick sweet cream, i.e. not sour, is we think preferable to clotted cream for this dish. The sauce should be of a good consistency and a dessert spoonful of flour will be needed for a large dish of the stew and from one and a half to two ounces of butter. The size of the fish must determine the precise quantity of liquid and of seasoning which they will require.

FROM *MODERN COOKERY FOR THE USE OF PRIVATE FAMILIES* BY ELIZA ACTON, 1845

It has been claimed that this book is one of the best cookery books in the English language. Eliza was born in 1799 in Sussex, the daughter of a brewer. She suffered from poor health as a young girl and was taken abroad to Paris. She returned to England eventually and started writing poetry. Many of her poems were published but one publisher refused her, saying there was no market for poetry written by maiden ladies and it would be better 'if you wrote a good, sensible cookbook'. She took his advice.

It took her four years to collect the recipes. She tried them out on her friends and finally, when she was 46, it was published. It was an instant bestseller with three editions published in the first year. Eliza was not a pretentious cook. Her recipes were always easy to follow and always delicious. She is rumoured to be the first cookery writer who listed ingredients separately from instructions in her books. She died in 1859 and was buried in Hampstead Parish Churchyard in London.

eel-pie island pie

Eel-pie Island is just off Twickenham on the Thames. Now most famous as the home of rock star Pete Townshend of The Who, the island used to be renowned for the pies sold there, which

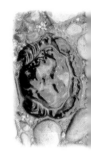

were thoroughly enjoyed by Londoners who came to have fun by the river. The island was then named after the pies.

Skin, clean and bone two Thames eels. Cut them in pieces and chop two small shallots. Pass the shallots in butter for five minutes [fry gently on hob] *and then add to them a small faggot* [bunch] *of parsley chopped with nutmeg, pepper and salt and two glasses of sherry. In the midst of this, deposit the eels, add enough water to cover them and set them on the fire to boil. When boiling point is reached, take out the pieces of eel and arrange them in a pie dish. In the meantime, add to the sauce two ounces of butter kneaded with two ounces of flour and let them incorporate by stirring over the fire. Finish the sauce with the juice of a whole lemon and pour it over the pieces of eel in the pie-dish. Some slices of hard-boiled egg may be cunningly arranged on the top and in it among the lower strata. Roof the whole with puff pastry; bake it for an hour. And lo! A pie worthy of Eel-Pie Island. It is a great question debated for ages on Richmond Hill whether this pie is best hot or cold. It is perfect either way.*

FROM *THE COOK'S ORACLE* BY DR WILLIAM KITCHINER, 1843

Dr Kitchiner's father made a fortune selling coal so was able to send his son to Eton, then University, and then to leave him a great deal of money. William trained for a medical degree in Glasgow, which in those days meant he could not practise in London. So he dedicated himself to science – and to entertaining his friends and generally having a good time. He wrote on optics and telescopes and he spent a lot of time experimenting with cooking with the help of Henry Osbourne, cook to Sir Joseph Banks.

His books are full of fun, asides and comments and he was passionate about food. He enjoyed preparing feasts for his friends and his luncheons were legendary, although only a few carefully chosen acquaintances were invited, making the invitation itself very treasured indeed. He died of a heart attack in 1827 – after dining with a friend.

CHAPTER 6

Flat Fish

I f you're ever in Whitstable or, next-door Seasalter, or anywhere around the muddy East Kent coast, you can try fishing without even a line. Just walk out on the mud flats when the tide is rushing in, keep your eyes peeled on the water and you might just see a few flat fish coming in with the tide. Of course, catching them is tricky – they're fast – and you'll probably end up face down in 5 inches of water but it's good fun trying.

The fish you're most likely to catch is the dab: a little flat fish which people think is a baby plaice but in fact is a whole species of its own. Its skin is actually rougher than that of the plaice, and many say the flesh is sweeter although this is debatable. Either way, they are delicious fried in butter, or grilled plain with butter and black pepper. Some dabs can grow to as big as half a kilo but you'll rarely find one bigger than that.

Then there is **plaice** – as good, some say, as the ones caught off the Sussex coast, **sole**, which is a beautiful delicate fish, **Dover sole**, **lemon sole** and **flounder**.

Dover soles were so-named because they used to be caught in great numbers off the coast of Dover. They used to love the Thames estuary too but we don't get so many of them now and many of the best Dover soles are caught off Rye and the Sussex coast. The Dover sole is a flat but long fish with a tough skin and is especially delicious – you don't need to do much with a Dover sole to enjoy it except use a little lemon juice, butter and seasoning.

The lemon sole is a lovely fish, but is considered to be a little less chic and flavoursome than the Dover sole. Its skin is more mottled than the spotted plaice and it doesn't carry as much flesh. Many of the best are caught off Folkestone.

The **flounder** – a kind of cross between a dab and a plaice – is an acquired taste. Caught in deep water they can be delicious but often enjoy life lying just off the mud flats and some describe their flesh as tasting a bit 'earthy' as a result. However, they are excellent in fish soup. Probably for that reason, the fishermen from Belgium, where they consume vast quantities of fish soup, love them. Years ago these men used to come over and catch their flounders off our shores. On the way home they would hang them up on a line on deck, the salty air drying and preserving them as they went. By the time they got home they were well preserved ready to be soaked in water and used in stews or thrown straight in the soup pot.

Turbot are sometimes found too, although they don't much like the estuary and prefer the deeper waters of the Channel. **Halibut** can still be caught if luck holds.

There are all sorts of ways you can cook flat fish. On the bone they're best used

plainly and quickly grilled with butter. But fillet them and you are spoiled for choice. Delia's favourite way with plaice fillets is to put them in an old-fashioned soup bowl, add butter, salt, pepper and a good splash of milk. Put another plate on top then steam the whole lot over a pan of boiling water for just a few minutes. Serve with their juice and some well-mashed potatoes. Good, comforting nursery food.

Skate are usually called roakers on the East Kent coast although you're unlikely to find them called that anywhere else. There are plenty of skate around these waters but they're not popular with fishermen as they're vicious creatures with serious spikes. The local ones are also called thorn-backed rays – another East Kent expression. Other rays, which swim further afield, are smooth-backed – these aren't roakers but plain skate – but if you encountered either in the sea they would be a frightening and grim sight.

By contrast, they are very beautiful to eat. So, at the fishmonger's, don't be put off by the sight of a whole skate displayed, as opposed to just the wings, which are what the chef uses for cooking. Skate wings are very meaty and easy to cook. Don't worry about all those bones – there's an easy art to eating skate. You simply scrape the flesh towards you with your

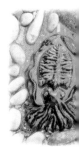

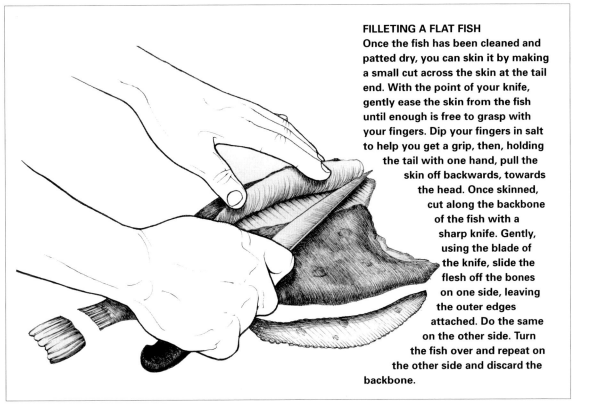

FILLETING A FLAT FISH
Once the fish has been cleaned and patted dry, you can skin it by making a small cut across the skin at the tail end. With the point of your knife, gently ease the skin from the fish until enough is free to grasp with your fingers. Dip your fingers in salt to help you get a grip, then, holding the tail with one hand, pull the skin off backwards, towards the head. Once skinned, cut along the backbone of the fish with a sharp knife. Gently, using the blade of the knife, slide the flesh off the bones on one side, leaving the outer edges attached. Do the same on the other side. Turn the fish over and repeat on the other side and discard the backbone.

the oyster seekers

knife, then turn the wing over and do the same on the other side. It's a neat and fulfilling operation.

The classic way to eat skate is with a beurre noisette – black butter – simply butter that has been melted to the browning stage together with lemon juice and capers. Skate was born to go with capers.

A green sauce is even better: prepare a large frying pan by warming with a good slice of butter plus a good dash of oil. Add some drained capers and black pepper then put your floured skate wings into the pan and fry gently for about 2 minutes – up to 5 if the wings are large. Add some fresh, chopped watercress and, as it's wilting, turn the wings over and cook for another couple of minutes. Add a little splash of white wine and maybe just a dash of vinegar. Serve immediately. Both the fish and the sauce are rich and filling so you'll need only plain new potatoes and maybe a green salad and a vegetable like plain green beans to go with it. Delicious.

the oyster seekers

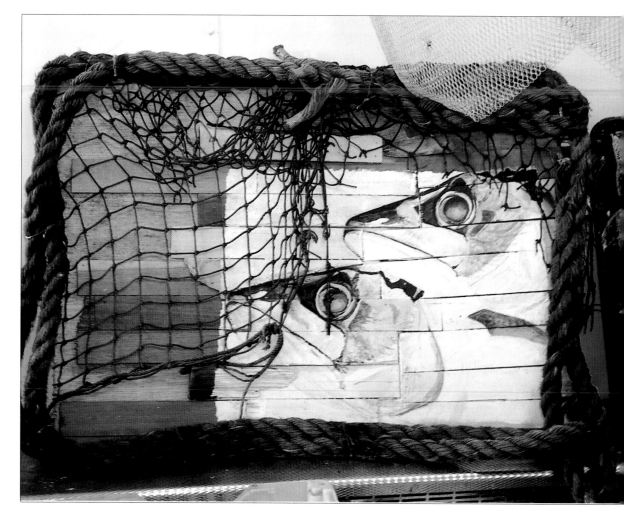

Roasted Skate Wing with Basil Pomme Purée and Baked Vine Tomatoes Served with Baked Lemon, Caper and Nut-Brown Butter Dressing

ingredients

Serves 4

4 skinned skate wings weighing about 250g each

450g potatoes, peeled and quartered

2 bunches of basil

1 lemon

84g butter and 1 tsp Savora sweet mustard

2 tsp capers

2 tsp parsley

4 small bunches of cherry tomatoes on the vine

75–100ml extra virgin oil

75–100ml double cream

good knob of butter

Bring the potatoes to the boil, simmer until just tender, drain and return to the pan to dry. Pass the potatoes through a fine sieve, place in a clean bowl, add the butter and the warmed cream, mix thoroughly and add the seasoning. Pick over the basil leaves and blanch in boiling salted water until vibrant green. Refresh immediately in ice-cold water, then squeeze dry and purée in a food processor, adding a little oil to make a fine purée. Pass this through a fine sieve and add to the potato purée. This will flavour it and give it the vibrant green colour.

Cut the lemon in half and bake in the oven with a little oil for 8 to 10 minutes until caramelised. Remove the lemon and allow to cool. Evenly season the skate. Cut each skate wing in half and pan-fry in butter until golden on both sides – this should take just a couple of minutes. Put in a pre-heated oven at 190ºC for 5 to 6 minutes depending on the size of the wings, saving the butter in the pan. Put the tomatoes in a baking tray, drizzle over a little oil and bake in the oven. Squeeze the juice from the lemons, add the capers, mustard, salt, pepper and the nut-brown butter. Whisk in the oil.

To serve, place a little basil mash at the centre of each plate, put the skate wing on top, add a little more mash, then the other half of the skate wing. Put the roasted tomatoes on top and then pour over the dressing.

the oyster seekers

Braised Skate Cheek with a Fennel, Apple and Walnut Salad

ingredients

Serves 4

500g fresh skate cheeks
1 carrot, finely diced
1 stick celery, finely diced
½ leek, finely diced
1 clove garlic, finely chopped
1 shallot, finely diced
1 bay leaf
few sprigs of thyme
2000ml chicken stock
75g plain flour
75g cornflour
1 bottle sparkling water
1–2 tsp five spice
2 Florence fennel
1 Pink Lady apple
100g fresh walnuts
200ml white wine
another 50–100ml white wine
2 star anise
few coriander seeds
few coriander leaves
juice of half a lemon
50ml sour cream
splash of good olive oil
oil for frying

the oyster seekers

Ask your fishmonger to remove the cheeks from the fish. Also ask him to remove any tiny pieces of white fish sinew. Wash the cheeks and then allow them to drain in order to remove any excess water.

Place the carrot, leek, garlic, celery and shallots into a hot pan with a little butter. Allow them to sweat for a few minutes without allowing them to brown. Add the 200ml wine and heat through until it is reduced by half.

Add approx 1000ml of hot stock to the mixture. Bring to the boil. Add the thyme and bay leaf and allow them to infuse for a few minutes. Add the skate cheeks, cover with greaseproof and place in a medium oven for about 30 minutes. Once removed from the oven, allow to go cold. Ideally, you should allow the skate cheeks to infuse overnight in the braising liquid.

Remove and discard the stalk and any tough outer pieces from the fennel. Keep and set aside any fronds of fresh fennel. Bring the remaining stock to the boil, season and add the star anise, coriander seeds and 50-100ml white wine. Gently poach the fennel until tender. Remove and allow to go cold.

Cut the fennel in half, remove the core and finely slice. Mix in any fronds of fennel you set aside earlier, along with some sliced apple, fresh walnuts and coriander. Drizzle with a little lemon juice and some good olive oil. Season with some salt and pepper. Allow to marinate at room temperature for about an hour.

To finish the dish, make the batter by mixing the two flours together, along with the five spice. Use as much or as little five spice as you like, depending on the strength

A whole raw skate

of flavour you want to achieve. Whisk in the sparkling water to create the batter.

Remove the cheeks from the liquid and carefully remove any excess moisture. Place in the batter and deep fry at 170ºC. Place on a plate along with the fennel salad and finish with a small spoonful of sour cream.

the oyster seekers

the oyster seekers

Baked Fillets of Brill Coated with a Cep Caviar Served with a Buttered Vine Tomato Sauce

ingredients

Serves 4

4 brill fillets weighing about 225g each

5 medium fennel bulbs, cleaned and quartered

2 cloves of garlic, puréed

3 sprigs of tarragon

olive oil, sea salt and pepper

a little fish or chicken stock

450g ceps

2 shallots, diced

another 2 cloves of garlic, chopped

50ml brandy

50ml Pernod

a punnet of ripe cherry tomatoes

325g cold, unsalted butter

28g chopped parsley

lemon juice

Let 100g of the butter come to room temperature and then mix with the garlic purée and chopped parsley. Add a squeeze of lemon juice and season lightly. Put in clingfilm, roll up like a sausage, and allow to firm in the fridge.

Brush off any mud from the ceps with a damp cloth, remove any tough bits of stalk and cut into even-sized pieces. Put a little butter in a pan and gently fry the shallots with the chopped garlic until they colour lightly, then flambé with the brandy. Add the ceps, and continue to cook over a high heat until lightly coloured. Season with salt and pepper. If it gets too dry add a little stock. Put the whole lot in a food processor and blend until puréed. Return to the pan and cook until any excess moisture has evaporated. Pass through a sieve and season.

Take the quartered fennel and caramelise in a pan by frying with a little oil. Transfer to a baking tray lined with foil, distribute evenly around the tray, season with salt and pepper, pour over a little olive oil, add the tarragon sprigs and a little Pernod, and cook until tender for 30 minutes in a preheated oven at 170ºC.

Remove the tops from the tomatoes and then blend them in a food processor. Pour through a sieve into a pan. Put on to simmer, season and add the cold butter piece by piece until the sauce thickens. Don't let it boil. Season the brill fillets, spread with your cep caviar and bake in a preheated oven for 8 to 10 minutes. To serve, place the roasted fennel in the centre of the plate, top with the cooked brill and pour a little of the tomato sauce around.

Pot-Roasted Turbot Studded with Pancetta and Sweet Garlic Served with Wilted Spinach and Caramelised Autumn Vegetables

ingredients

Serves 4

4 x 225g tronchons of turbot
('steaks' of fish)
52g pancetta, cut into lardons
8 cloves of sweet garlic
225g spinach leaves
16 baby onions
450g salsify
half a celeriac, cut into 1cm dice
100ml olive oil
225g unsalted butter
500ml chicken stock
100ml double cream
100ml white wine
56g capers
56g coriander
a few sprigs of lemon thyme,
nutmeg, salt, pepper

Make a small incision either end of the turbot steaks and stud with the pancetta and sweet garlic. Pour over a little olive oil, cover in clingfilm and put in the fridge. Pick over the spinach leaves, removing any thick stalks. Wash two or three times to remove any dirt, then blanch in a little boiling salted water until vibrant green – this should take about 2 minutes. Refresh the spinach immediately in cold water. Squeeze out all the water and put to one side. Peel the baby onions, put in a hot pan with some olive oil, and cook until they caramelise (go a little brown). Then add enough stock to come a quarter of the way up the level of the onions, a knob of butter, the lemon thyme, season with sea salt and cook until just tender.

Peel the salsify and immediately place into acidic water (water with lemon juice). Then cut into 5-inch batons and, in a pan, just cover with boiling water and add a knob of butter. Season, cook until just tender, then drain and allow to cool naturally. Put the diced celeriac in a hot pan with olive oil, along with a little of the thyme, and cook until just tender and golden brown. Moisten with a little of the stock if you think it's getting too dry. Heat a sauteuse pan with olive oil, season the turbot steaks with salt and pepper, and cook until golden brown, turning once. Add the onions, the salsify, a good knob of butter and the celeriac. Again, moisten with a little stock if you feel it's too dry. Put the whole lot in a preheated oven at 200ºC and cook for about 8 minutes, basting when you can with the melted butter in the pan. Put the fish and the garnish on a tray to rest for a couple of minutes while you deglaze the pan with a little white wine and reduce to nothing. Add some of the chicken stock to the pan, the juice of 1 lemon and carry on reducing down by two-thirds. Add the double cream and whisk in 125g of cold butter. The sauce should be nice and rich and of a consistency thick enough to coat a spoon. Add the capers and the finely chopped coriander. Reheat the spinach with a little butter, salt and pepper and nutmeg. To dress the plate, put the spinach in the centre of the plate, top with a turbot steak and some salsify, spread the onions and celeriac around the plate and pour a little sauce around the plate.

127

Pan-Fried Halibut Set on a Fresh Pea and Pancetta Risotto and Finished with a Horseradish Cream

ingredients

Serves 4

4 halibut fillets weighing about
   225g each
250g of risotto rice (Arborio)
125g pancetta
225g tub of crème fraiche
2 tbsp horseradish sauce
a pinch of cayenne
a squeeze of lemon juice
225g fresh peas
an additional 150g fresh peas
75g butter
2 medium shallots, finely diced
1 clove garlic, finely diced
1600ml of chicken stock
26g Parmesan
100ml white wine
olive oil

Pod the peas and put them to one side – put the pea shells into three pints of chicken stock and bring to the boil. Allow to simmer for 35 minutes. Pass through some muslin, which you can buy at any haberdasher's and after cooking you simply wash it out well and reuse. After simmering, the stock should have reduced to about two pints.

Sweat the shallots in a little butter, add 25g of the fresh peas and add a little stock. Cook for 5 minutes until the peas are a vibrant green and tender. Season with salt and pepper. Purée in a food processor, then pass through a fine sieve. Blanch the remainder of the peas in boiling salted water, and then drain and refresh in cold water. Cut the pancetta into lardons and slowly fry in a little olive oil until golden and crispy.

Melt 26g of the butter in a large saucepan. Add the diced shallot and garlic and lightly fry for 3 minutes without allowing to brown. Add the rice and cook for another couple of minutes, making sure all the rice is coated with the butter. Add the wine and stir continuously until all the liquid is absorbed. Add the stock a ladle at a time, stirring continuously, until it has all been absorbed and the rice is nice and tender but not mushy. Just before the risotto is ready, season the halibut fillets and pan-fry in a hot pan until golden, turn over, add a knob of butter and continue to cook the halibut, basting all the time until firm to the touch. In a bowl, mix the crème fraiche with the horseradish, lemon juice, salt, pepper and cayenne. To finish the risotto, add the pea purée, blanched peas and Parmesan, the pancetta and season. Mix evenly.

To serve, place the risotto in a 3½-inch ring, place the halibut on top, surround with some of the horseradish sauce and eat immediately. You can do without the ring if you wish but it looks better with it.

Halibut are sometimes still found in the Thames Estuary

Glazed Lemon Sole Fillets Topped with a Tomato and Cucumber Salsa and Finished with Hollandaise Sauce

ingredients

Serves 4

4 whole lemon soles weighing
    about 225g each

half a cucumber

4 plum tomatoes, peeled,
    blanched and deseeded

20g fresh ginger, peeled and
    finely diced

some fresh coriander leaves,
    chopped

1 yellow pepper

half portion of hollandaise
    (see page 193)

half portion of herb oil (see page
    197)

mixed salad leaves

a few fresh herbs: perhaps
    chervil, tarragon and chive
    batons

FOR THE TOMATO FONDUE:

1400g plum tomatoes, blanched
    peeled and deseeded

2 shallots, finely diced

2 cloves of garlic

a few sprigs of lemon thyme

4 tbsp vinaigrette

Make the hollandaise sauce and keep warm. Make the herb oil and keep refrigerated.

Remove the heads from the fish and fillet, removing the skin – or get your fishmonger to do this for you. Fold the fillets in half, cover and put in the fridge.

Finely dice the shallots and sweat with the garlic and a little olive oil, without browning. Add the tomatoes and the lemon thyme, and season. Keep cooking very slowly for about an hour, until you have your tomato fondue. The reason the fondue takes so long to cook is because you want the tomatoes to completely collapse, concentrating all the flavour.

Grill the yellow pepper with a little olive oil until the skin blackens all over. Place in a bowl and cover with clingfilm. Leave for 5 minutes. You will then be able to peel off the bitter skin easily. Deseed the pepper and dice finely. Finely dice the 4 plum tomatoes. Peel, core and dice the cucumber. Put the cucumber with the pepper and diced tomato in a bowl with the ginger and coriander, season and lightly mix. Add enough hollandaise to bind them all together.

Put a little of the salsa on each piece of fish and bake in a preheated oven at 180ºC until the fish is cooked through and the salsa nice and glazed.

To serve: reheat the tomato fondue and place a small

amount on each plate. Divide the fish fillets between the plates. Add the herbs to the salad, dress with vinaigrette and arrange on top of the fish. Add a drizzle of herb oil.

This works very well as a barbecue dish.

Lemon-Scented Plaice Fillets Stuffed with Fresh Langoustine Served with Ricola and Cherry Tomato Salad

ingredients

Serves 4

4 whole medium plaice, skinned
    and filleted
1 whole lemon
16 fresh langoustine, peeled
2 bulbs of fennel
2 packets of ricola salad –
    ricola is very much like rocket
    but with smaller leaves
16 cherry tomatoes, red
    and yellow
56g fresh Parmesan
good pinch of saffron
400g Anya potatoes
2 pints chicken stock
a few sprigs of dill
butter
splash of white wine
285ml chicken stock
4 large sheets of foil
4 large sheets greaseproof paper
3 tbsp balsamic vinegar

Peel the potatoes, cover with the chicken stock, top up with a little water if needed, add the saffron and cook until tender. Drain and allow to cool. Prepare the papillottes according to the diagram on page 61. When they're ready, re-open the greaseproof and then the foil and lightly grease the foil with some butter.

Peel off the outside of the fennel, removing any tough strands. Cut in half, remove the core and finely slice. Put the fennel in a frying pan with a little oil, lightly fry until slightly coloured. Season, moisten with a little wine and stock and allow to simmer until tender. Remove the fennel and allow to cool. Slice the lemon and divide the slices between the pieces of foil along with the fennel. Evenly slice the potatoes and divide those too. Take the langoustine and roll the plaice fillets around them. Lightly season and place on top of the potatoes. Pick over the dill and evenly sprinkle a little over the fish. Then add a little wine and stock to moisten the package. Seal the papillottes, tightly folding over the edges.

Bake the papillottes in a preheated oven at 230ºC for about 10 to 12 minutes depending on the thickness of the fish. Make the dressing by whisking the balsamic vinegar with the olive oil, and lightly season. Pick over the ricola, cut up the cherry tomatoes, dress with the dressing and finish with Parmesan shavings. Serve the papillottes with the salad on the side. Cut open the papillottes and smell the sea.

Whole Dover Sole Layered with Asparagus and Hollandaise Sauce

ingredients

Serves 4

4 whole Dover sole, between
   500g and 670g each
16 spears of asparagus
1 portion of hollandaise
   (see page 193)
650g Jersey Royals
mixed salad leaves
a pinch of chervil
a few tarragon leaves
a few chive batons (chopped
   lengthways) and 2 tsp finely
   chopped chives
100ml balsamic vinaigrette
knob of butter

Make the hollandaise sauce and set aside, covered. Make the vinaigrette by whisking olive oil with balsamic vinegar and adding salt and pepper.

Bring the Jersey Royals to the boil and simmer until tender. Drain, place in a bowl and pour over the vinaigrette while still warm – they absorb the flavour beautifully that way. Peel and blanch the asparagus in boiling water for 1 minute, then drain and refresh in cold water. Pick over the salad leaves, wash and dry thoroughly. Add the chervil, tarragon and chive batons and leave in the fridge until needed.

Prepare and fillet the sole according to the diagram on page 119. For this recipe, when you reach the final stage of filleting and have made an incision into the sole, head to tail, with the point of your knife, release the left side of the fillet so that it is still attached to the fish, i.e. so it opens like a book. Repeat with the fillet on the other side of the fish so you end up with two 'books'.

Lightly season the sole, place on a greased tray and grill for 8 to 10 minutes. Remove from the grill and sandwich the asparagus between the fillets adding a good spread of hollandaise sauce. Grill until golden brown. Put a knob of butter in a pan along with a little water, add the Jersey Royals and reheat them, waiting until the butter and water have reduced enough just to give the potatoes a good coating. Lightly season and finish with chopped chives.

Present the fish on a plate with a portion of potatoes, a lightly dressed salad and garnish with a good wedge of lemon.

the oyster seekers

Grilled Dabs with a Purée of Cannellini Beans, Surrounded by Wild Mushrooms and a Lemon Butter Sauce

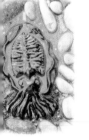

ingredients

Serves 4

8 whole dabs weighing about
    250g each
200g cannellini beans
half a leek
half a carrot
1 stick of celery
a bay leaf and a sprig
    of thyme
6 cloves of garlic
a quarter of a bunch of flat
    leaf parsley
1 tsp curly parsley
300g wild mushrooms – others
    will do but wild are much better
1 shallot, finely diced
1 lemon
250g butter, cut into cubes
another 50g butter
olive oil, salt and pepper

Soak the beans in water for 24 hours, drain and place in a clean pan with the leek, carrot, celery, bay leaf and 6 cloves of garlic. Cover with water. Bring the beans and water to the boil and boil hard for 5 minutes. Turn down the heat and simmer until the beans are tender. Remove the vegetables but leave in the garlic, strain the beans and keep the bean liquid. Purée the beans with the garlic in a food processor, pass through a fine sieve, and finish off by mixing in 50g of butter, salt and pepper to taste and the roughly chopped flat leaf parsley.

Prepare the wild mushrooms by removing any mud with a damp cloth and removing any bits of damaged stalk. If the mushrooms are large, break into even-sized pieces, or keep them whole if they're small. Quickly sauté the mushrooms in a little oil, then drain them and leave to cool. Remove the head of the dabs but cutting as close to the head as possible. Run the fish under cold water, removing any blood clots or remaining intestines. Dry the fish and lightly score the top of it (this allows the heat to penetrate evenly). Place the dabs on a greased tray and lightly season with salt and pepper and put in a preheated oven at 190ºC for 8 minutes. Lightly sweat the shallots and garlic in butter and add the mushrooms. Cook for about 2 minutes, season, remove and finish off with chopped parsley. To make the sauce, take the bean stock, add the juice of one lemon, seasoning and the cubed butter over a gentle heat while whisking. Keep the sauce warm but don't boil because it could separate. Put the dabs on the plate with a spoonful of cannellini purée, a few wild mushrooms and some of the lemon sauce. Garnish with the chopped curly parsley.

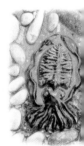

the oyster seekers

CHAPTER 7

Round Fish

round fish

Cod and **haddock** both like cold water, and need it to spawn, so most cod is fished in deep waters. Cod has become fashionable again as it's becoming harder to obtain – the waters are being over fished and are getting warmer, forcing the fish further and further north for spawning. The fishermen therefore follow them. Local cod and haddock are still available – haddock especially off the south coast – and are superb. **Codlings** – small cod – can be caught closer to shore. 'You know they're around because they eat all the shrimps,' says Delia.

Local **seabass** is delicious. It has been caught as close as 25 metres from The Street, the mile-long spit of sand and shingle which juts into the sea beyond the harbour. It is often caught close to wrecks. Seabass used to be called 'salmon bass' because it is big and silvery. School bass is smaller and, if you're lucky, you can find it swimming in big shoals.

'The seabass is a greedy fish and grows large,' says Delia. 'It's also got excellent eyesight and it's clever – you'll rarely fool it with a plain hook. You need a very thin, almost translucent line and a spinner: a little imitation "fish", maybe made of Dover sole skin. That swivels around in the water so it appears to be swimming.

'My mother used to wrap the whole fish in greaseproof paper and steam it or bake it in the oven. One of my favourite ways to eat sea bass – very fresh seabass – is to cut the flesh into quarter-inch pieces and marinade it for 12–24 hours in fresh lime or lime and lemon juice. Drain and eat with a side salad and bread. The acidity of the juice breaks down the fibres in the fish and "cooks" it.'

Some very big **monkfish** have been caught locally. They're large and ugly, blackish or gunmetal grey in colour and they have big mouths with lots of little, sharp teeth. But looks aren't everything. The tail is where the meat is – there's no meat on the rest of it – and the flesh is very firm and tasty.

to salt cod

Salted cod is a national dish in Portugal where they call it baccalau, and it's popular elsewhere too. Salting is an ideal way to preserve the fish in a hot climate and, if you've never tried it, you may be surprised to know it doesn't taste as salty as you'd imagine, at least no more than other fish. It does take time but this is how we salt cod in the restaurant. Wash the fish, pat it dry, then put it on a bed of salt – a lot of it, enough to cover the base of the baking dish. Then cover it very thoroughly with more salt so you can't see the cod at all. Leave it for 24 hours but, as often as you can, drain off the moisture the salt has drawn out of the fish, pat it dry and add more salt. Eventually the cod will go as hard as a board. Before you want to use it, soak in cold water for at least a day, changing the water frequently.

Most cod is fished in deep water.

Grilled Tuna with a Creamy Horseradish Mash and French Beans Tossed in Red Wine Vinegar

ingredients

Serves 4

fresh horseradish or a jar of good
   shop-bought creamed
   horseradish
750g potatoes, peeled and
   quartered
4 portions of fresh yellow fin tuna
   weighing about 225g each
250g french beans
1 small tub crème fraiche
squeeze of lemon juice
salt, pepper and cayenne
2 plum tomatoes, blanched,
   quartered and deseeded
100ml fresh cream
1 to 2 tbsp red wine
   vinegar
good knob of butter

Bring the potatoes to the boil in lightly salted water and simmer until tender. Drain and return the potatoes to the pan to dry out. Pass the potatoes through a fine sieve into a clean bowl. Bring the cream to the boil and add enough horseradish to give a good flavour – some like it hotter than others. Allow to infuse for a few minutes, then add to the potatoes. Mix thoroughly, adding the butter and extra seasoning to taste. Keep the horseradish mash warm.

Put half the crème fraiche into a bowl and add the lemon juice, salt and cayenne. Mix thoroughly then add the diced tomato and crush into the crème fraiche using a fork.

Cook the beans in boiling salted water until tender. Drain and put in a bowl with the red wine vinegar, allow to infuse for a few minutes, then mix in the crème fraiche mixture and check the seasoning. Season the tuna and cook for 2 minutes either side in a very hot griddle pan. Allow the tuna to rest for a few minutes before serving.

To serve: put a good helping of horseradish mash in the centre of the plate, cut the tuna fillets in half and put a half either side of the mash. Top with the french beans and crème fraiche mixture.

Roasted Cod on a Ragout of Creamed Cabbage Finished with Wild Mushrooms and Crispy Bacon and Served with Steamed Mussels and a Light Pea Veloute

ingredients

Serves 4

4 fresh cod fillets weighing
about 225g each

500g Savoy cabbage, finely
shredded

225g mixed wild mushrooms

200g unsmoked back bacon

2 shallots, finely diced

150g fresh peas

half portion of fish cream sauce
(see page 186)

20 live mussels

25g diced carrot

25g diced shallot

15g chopped garlic

56g unsalted butter

3 tbsp cold water

100ml double cream

lemon juice

Blanch the cabbage in boiling salted water for 4 minutes. Refresh in cold water to stop the cooking process and keep the colour. Squeeze out any excess water. For the pea purée: sweat the shallots in butter, making sure that they don't brown. Add the fresh peas and water, and lightly season. When the peas are bright green and tender, purée in a food processor. Now pass through a sieve and place in the freezer until just cold – this keeps the colour vibrant.

Prepare the mushrooms by removing any dirt with a damp cloth. Never wash mushrooms under a running tap or in cold water, as they will retain the water. Remove the ends of the stalks. If the mushrooms are small keep whole, if very large carefully break into smaller pieces.

Put the mussels into cold water and discard any that float. Remove any barnacles or beards. Trim the skin from the pancetta and cut into lardons about 1cm thick. Fry in olive oil until crispy and golden. Drain on a kitchen towel. Sauté the mushrooms in a little olive oil and, when they are lightly cooked, strain in a colander, allowing any moisture to drain away.

Sweat the shallot, carrot and garlic with a little oil in a separate pan, add the mushrooms and heat gently for a few minutes. Add the cabbage, season to taste and add

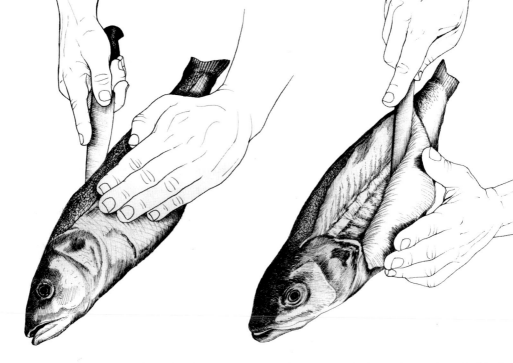

PREPARING AND FILLETING A ROUND FISH
First trim, gut and clean the fish. Scaly fish like mullet and herring need to be de-scaled too. To do this, hold the fish firmly by the tail over some paper – the scales tend to fly everywhere – and working towards the head, scrape off the scales with the back of your knife. Now gut the fish, trim the fins and tail and remove the head if you wish. Wash and pat dry. The fish is now ready to be cooked whole but if you want to fillet it, start by laying it on a board with the tail towards you. Insert the knife just behind the head until you find the backbone, then, holding the fish steady in the palm of your hand, slice along the backbone from head to tail. Keep the knife as close to the bone as you can and gently slice down until you can lift off the whole fillet. Turn the fish over and repeat, resting it on the first fillet which makes removing the second fillet easier.

the cream – you might not need all of it. The cream will slowly thicken and, when the sauce is as thick as you want it, add the bacon. Turn off the heat and keep warm.

Season the fish and quickly fry it gently in oil, skin-side down, for a couple of minutes, until the skin is golden brown. Then put it in the oven with a knob of butter for about 8 minutes. Baste frequently. Now bring the sauce back to the boil, add the mussels, wait for them to open in the heat then remove them from the sauce and place around the plate. (Mark keeps them in their shells.) Finish the sauce by adding some of the pea purée, enough to give a good green colour. Add a squeeze of lemon. To dress the plate, put the ragout in the centre, the cod on top, surround with the mussels and then with the sauce.

Local Smoked Haddock Rested on Bubble and Squeak and Glazed with Welsh Rarebit

This is a wonderful combination: a Whitstable haddock, Mark's bubble and squeak and Welsh rarebit from a Gary Rhodes recipe.

ingredients

Serves 4

2 undyed haddock fillets smoked, descaled and pin boned (i.e. bones removed)

1kg potatoes, peeled and quartered – Desiree or Maris Piper are best

400g shredded cabbage

2 bunches of spring onions, peeled and finely diced

100ml goose or duck fat, melted

a quarter of a portion of Welsh rarebit (see page 196)

a quarter portion of fish sauce (see page 186)

1 tbsp grainy mustard

26g butter

52g flour

1 tsp chopped chives, salt, pepper and nutmeg

4 metal rings

Make the Welsh rarebit and allow to cool. Put the shredded cabbage into a baking tray, pour over the melted goose fat and lightly season. Cover with foil and cook in a preheated oven at 150ºC for about 45 minutes, mixing occasionally. Make the fish sauce and set aside.

Put the potatoes in cold water and bring to the boil, lightly seasoning with salt. Cook until tender, drain and return to the pan to dry. Pass the potatoes through a fine sieve into a bowl and allow to cool. Add the cabbage to the potatoes along with some of the fat.

Sweat the spring onions in butter for a few minutes, add to the cabbage mixture, mix thoroughly, season and add a small pinch of nutmeg. Cut the haddock into four pieces weighing about 225g each. Spread each with some Welsh rarebit, put in a greased tray and bake in the oven at 200ºC for about 8 minutes until the fish is just cooked. Flash the fish under the grill for about a minute to create a nice glaze.

Fill the metal rings with bubble and squeak and lightly dust both sides with flour. Fry in a little hot oil until golden brown – then put in the oven for another 8 minutes, turning occasionally. Bring the fish sauce to the boil, add the mustard and mix in the chopped chives.

To serve: place the glazed haddock on top of a ring of hot bubble and squeak and surround with the fish sauce.

A Cassoulet of Seabass with Celeriac Fondants

ingredients

Serves 4

2 fillets of seabass weighing
    about 500g each, descaled and
    pin boned (i.e. bone removed)
500g haricots blanc
1500ml chicken stock, plus
    another 600ml chicken stock
3 slices of Parma ham cut into
    thin strips
4 spring onions, cleaned, peeled
    and finely chopped
4 plum tomatoes, blanched
    deseeded, quartered and diced
2 tbsp chopped parsley
a few sprigs of chervil, roughly
    chopped
150g unsalted butter
1 medium celeriac
knob of butter
a mirepoix of half a leek, 1 carrot,
    1 onion, 4 cloves garlic, a few
    sprigs of thyme and a couple of
    bay leaves
16 pieces of asparagus, peeled
    and blanched

Soak the haricot beans in cold water for 24 hours then drain well. Put the beans in a pan and cover with chicken stock, add the mirepoix (mix of roughly chopped vegetables) and bring to the boil. Boil hard for 5 minutes then simmer for about 50 minutes until the beans are soft but still whole.

While the beans are cooking, make the celeriac fondants. Discard the outer layer of the celeriac. Trim it into oval shapes about 1½ cm thick. You will need eight ovals – two per portion. Take the butter slice it thinly and place all over the bottom of the pan. Add the celeriac, and heat until one side goes golden brown. Turn the celeriac and add the remaining stock. Bring back to the boil and allow to simmer until almost all the liquid has boiled away. The fondants should be nice and soft but still whole. Remove them from the heat and keep warm.

When the beans are cooked, remove them from the cooking stock, discard the vegetables and boil to reduce the stock by half. Add the knob of butter and cook until nicely emulsified. By now the sauce should be thickening slightly, so add the Parma ham, the spring onions, parsley, chervil and cook for another couple of minutes. Then add the beans and the diced tomato. Check the seasoning and keep warm.

Trim the seabass fillets and cut into 4 even-sized pieces weighing about 200g each. Score the skin evenly to prevent it from shrinking. Season the fish and place skin-side down in a hot pan and allow to caramelise in a little oil. Turn down the heat and cook the fish almost all the way through on its skin. Rewarm the fondants and the beans. Turn the fish over to cook the top of the fillets, which will not take long at all.

To dress the plate put the fondants in the centre, put the cooked seabass on top and evenly spoon the beans around these. Finally, pour over the cooking liquor, place the rewarmed asparagus on top of the fish and add a wedge of lemon.

145

Roasted Monkfish on Olive and Sun-Dried Tomato Mash Served with Crispy Fennel and a Coriander Pesto

ingredients

Serves 4

olive oil

800g potatoes – Maris Piper, Desiree or King Edward, if possible

115g whole pitted black olives, finely diced

115g sun-dried tomatoes, finely diced

100ml cream

85g unsalted butter

4 monkfish fillets weighing about 225g each

1 fennel bulb

110g cornflour

55g plain flour

some cold sparkling water

coriander pesto (see recipe page 196)

1000ml vegetable oil

To prevent the fish curling up during cooking, remove the grey membrane running along each fillet. Trim the fillets neatly then wrap them up in clingfilm and leave in the fridge for about an hour. Peel, quarter and cook the potatoes in boiling salted water until just tender. Drain and return to the pan to dry. Pass through a sieve into a clean bowl. While the potatoes are still hot, bring the cream to the boil and pour over the potatoes along with the diced butter, olives and tomatoes. Mix thoroughly. Taste and adjust your seasoning. Cover and keep warm.

Peel the fennel, removing the outer ribs and any tough pieces. Halve, remove the core, then finely slice into thin strips. Put the flour and cornflour into a bowl with a pinch of salt and slowly whisk in the sparkling water until you have a light batter (known as tempura). Put the fennel in the batter, turn on the fryer or heat the oil to 180ºC and fry until golden.

Heat some oil in a non-stick frying pan, season the monkfish with salt and pepper and cook presentation-side down until golden brown. Turn the monkfish, adding a knob of butter and baste while cooking for a couple of minutes. Place in a preheated oven for about 5 minutes. When the monkfish is cooked, remove from the oven and allow to rest for a couple of minutes.

Reheat the mash and cooked fennel. Put the mash in the centre of the plate, cut each monkfish fillet in half and place on the potatoes, put the deep-fried fennel on top and drizzle around a little coriander pesto.

Baked Hake with a Salsa Verdi Mash and Kentish Asparagus Wrapped in Parma Ham

ingredients

Serves 4

4 x 225g pieces of hake fillet
1lb potatoes
50g capers, chopped
50g gherkins, quartered and then
   thinly sliced
100ml olive oil
2 shallots, finely diced
1 bunch flat leaf parsley
half a lemon
12 asparagus
6 pieces of thinly sliced
   Parma ham

Peel, wash and boil the potatoes until tender. Drain and put them back in the pan. Return to the stove to dry out for a few minutes. Pass the potatoes through a fine sieve. Beat in a little butter and cream and season to taste. Pick, wash and roughly chop the parsley. Add the gherkins, capers and prepared parsley to the potato mash.

Place the shallots in a pan and just cover with the oil. Place over a gentle heat and allow to cook very slowly, for about an hour. When the shallots are nice and tender, drain off the oil and place the shallots into the potato mixture. Mix thoroughly.

Season the hake with salt and pepper. Place it skin-side down on a baking tray. Brush with melted butter and bake at 190ºC for about 8 minutes.

While the fish is cooking, blanch the asparagus in boiling, slated water until just tender. Refresh immediately and, when cold, pat dry and wrap the pancetta around the asparagus. Rewarm the mash, place on the plate and sit the fish on top. Drizzle over a little lemon.

Quickly pan-fry the asparagus with Parma ham until golden. Place on top of the fish arrangement and serve with a crisp salad.

the oyster seekers

Caramelised Salmon with a Lemon, Vanilla and Sesame Seed Crust Served on Pommes Lyonnaise, Roasted Asparagus and Piquillo Pepper Dressing

ingredients

Serves 4

4 salmon fillets weighing about
   225g each
50g toasted sesame seeds
1 portion of lemon and vanilla
   syrup (see page 198)
450g potatoes – preferably
   Charlotte potatoes because
   they're good and waxy
16 asparagus spears, cleaned and
   peeled
1 jar of piquillo peppers
50ml red wine vinegar
100ml olive oil
50ml groundnut oil
1 medium red onion
1 tbsp chopped parsley, knob of
   butter, salt, pepper, sugar and
   4 lemon wedges

Make the lemon and vanilla syrup and set aside. Wash the potatoes and cook in salted boiling water until just tender. Drain and allow to cool. Make the piquillo pepper dressing: whizz the drained peppers in a food processor, then pass through a fine sieve removing any seeds, add the vinegar with the salt, pepper and sugar and mix well. Slowly whisk in the oil until you have the consistency you like. If it gets too thick add a little hot water.

Blanch the prepared asparagus in boiling water for a minute, remove and immediately refresh in cold water to keep the colour. Slice the red onion thinly and sauté in olive oil until lightly coloured and cooked. Keep warm. Peel the potatoes and slice into even-sized pieces about 1cm thick. Season and sauté in a little olive oil until the edges are golden. Add a knob of butter and turn the potatoes. Carry on cooking until the potatoes are golden brown and crispy. Gently mix the potatoes with the onion, sprinkle with chopped parsley and keep warm.

Season the salmon and pan-fry, skin-side down, until it just starts to go golden. Put in a preheated oven at 180ºC for 3 minutes, turn, and cook for another 2 minutes.

Remove the fillets from the oven and spread each with some lemon syrup. Sprinkle on the sesame seeds and allow to rest for a couple of minutes, keeping warm.

While the salmon is having a rest, pan-fry the asparagus until lightly coloured and season lightly. To serve, place the potatoes and onions in the centre of the plate, put a salmon fillet on top, lean the asparagus against the salmon, spoon some dressing around the edge and serve with a lemon wedge.

Pan-Fried Fillets of John Dory with a Goat's Cheese and Basil Ratatouille Accompanied by Roasted Asparagus and White Bean Sauce

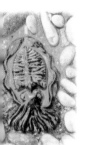

ingredients

Serves 4

4 fillets of John Dory weighing about 225g each

1 yellow and 1 red pepper, quartered and deseeded

1 aubergine

2 courgettes

1 onion

200ml double cream

200g goat's cheese

15 basil leaves, finely cut

225g white beans

half a leek

half a carrot

1 shallot

2 cloves of garlic

1 bay leaf

16 asparagus spears

a few chopped chives, lemon juice and salt and pepper to season

Soak the beans for 24 hours, drain, put in a clean pan with the leek, carrot, shallot, garlic and bay leaf, cover with cold water, bring to the boil and boil hard for 5 minutes. Simmer until the beans are tender.

To make the white bean sauce, remove the vegetables and the bay leaf, and strain the beans, keeping the bean stock. Blend the beans in a food processor until puréed, adding a little stock if you think it's getting too thick. Pass through a fine sieve and put back into a clean pan. Simmer, bring back to the boil adding some more stock, whisking all the time until you have a consistency that will coat a spoon. Season, finish with a squeeze of lemon, remove from the heat and put to one side.

For the ratatouille, cook the vegetables – aubergine, courgettes, peppers and onions – individually in a pan with some oil and seasoning. When they're tender put them together in a colander and allow to drain. Bring the cream to the boil and carry on boiling until it is reduced by half. Now remove the skin from the goat's cheese and grate the cheese into the cream so the cheese melts – but don't allow the mixture to boil. Put the drained vegetables into a bowl, pour over the cream and cheese mixture, add the basil, and mix thoroughly.

Peel the asparagus and blanch in boiling water for 1 minute then immediately refresh in cold water to keep the colour. Season the John Dory and pan-fry skin-side down until golden brown, turn the heat right down and allow to cook almost all the way through. At the last moment, turn the fish over to quickly cook on the top side. Remove the fish and keep warm.

Pan-fry the asparagus until lightly golden and season lightly. Rewarm the ratatouille and the sauce. Add a few chopped chives to the sauce.

To serve, place the ratatouille in the centre of the plate, put the John Dory on top along with the asparagus and pour the sauce around.

the oyster seekers

Pan-Fried Fillets of Red Mullet Topped with an Olive and Sun-Dried Tomato Tapenade Accompanied by a Celeriac Remoularde and Herb Oil

ingredients

Serves 4

4 whole red mullet weighing
   about 225g each, filleted
a quarter of a medium celeriac
1 tsp Dijon mustard
2 tbsp mayonnaise
a quarter of a bunch of coriander
lemon juice
one portion of herb oil (see recipe
   page 197)
some fresh chervil and chives
vinaigrette (see recipe page 198)
mixed salad leaves

FOR THE TAPENADE:
150g pitted black olives
26g sun-dried tomatoes
4 fresh anchovy fillets
100ml olive oil
1 clove garlic
26g pine kernels

First make the tapenade. Put the olives in a food processor, blend briefly and then add all the other ingredients until you have nice purée. Set aside.

Peel the celeriac and cut into wafer-thin slices using a mandolin, then cut the slices into julienne, i.e. really thin strips. Put the lemon juice, mustard, cayenne and salt into a bowl, mix thoroughly, fold the celeriac into the mayonnaise until all the pieces are coated.

Make the herb oil according to the recipe. Wash and dry the salad leaves, add the chervil and chives. Don't season the mullet fillets as the tapenade is quite salty. Just thinly spread some tapenade over each fillet, pan-fry for a few minutes skin-side down and finish off in the oven for a few minutes, keeping the fish skin-side down with the tapenade on top. Chop the coriander and fold into the celeriac mix.

To serve, put some celeriac mix into the centre of each plate, lay the hot mullet fillets across the top, dress the salad with vinaigrette and put a little on top of the mullet, and drizzle the herb oil around.

Glazed Smoked Salmon with Globe Artichokes and Poached Eggs

ingredients

Serves 4

4 globe artichokes
50g carrot, diced
50g leek, diced
50g celery, diced
sprig of thyme
1 bay leaf
100ml white wine
500ml chicken stock
1 clove of garlic, finely chopped
4 poached eggs
2 lemons
400g smoked salmon
1 portion hollandaise sauce (see
   recipe page 193)

Squeeze the lemons into a bowl of cold water. (This is to stop the artichokes from oxidising during preparation.) Prepare the artichoke by snapping off the stalk and then removing the outer leaves just far enough so as not to damage the artichoke. Cut away the excess leaves and you shoud be left with the hairy purple-coloured artichokes.

Find a pan that will be big enough to hold the 4 artichokes. Place the diced vegetables into the pan and allow them to sweat in a little butter for a few minutes. Add the wine and allow it to reduce by half. Add the hot stock, thyme and bay leaf. Allow to infuse and then add the artichokes. Cook until the artichokes are just tender.

While the artichokes are cooking, make the Hollandaise sauce. When the artichokes are cooked, remove them from the liquid and allow them to cool slightly. Take a metal spoon and gently scrape out the centre of the artichoke and place on a plate.

Bring a large pan of water to the boil and reduce to a simmer. Add a little vinegar and then poach the eggs. When they are cooked, place one in the centre of each artichoke. Lay the smoked salmon over the top, spoon over some Hollandaise sauce and glaze under the grill until slightly golden. Serve immediately.

the oyster seekers

Trout Forestière

ingredients

Serves 4

4 pieces of trout fillet weighing
    about 225g each
16 pieces of asparagus
4 thin slices of Parma ham
4 medium potatoes
1 litre chicken stock (see recipe
    page 189)
225g packet of butter
250g wild mushrooms
1 medium shallot, finely diced
1 clove garlic, finely chopped
1 tablespoon chopped parsley
olive oil, a few sprigs of thyme,
    salt and pepper to season

FOR THE DRESSING:
50ml lemon juice
50ml vegetable oil
100ml olive oil
1 tsp horseradish
1 tsp lightly chopped tarragon
1 tsp Savora mustard, salt and
    pepper

Peel the potatoes and cut into rounds about 2cm thick. Slice the butter lengthways and place in a cold pan big enough to hold the potatoes. Press the potatoes into the butter, put on a high heat and allow the butter to clarify. Carry on cooking until the potatoes are light brown around the bottom – don't lift the potatoes from the bottom of the pan. When the potato bottoms are golden, remove the pan from the heat, cover with a tea towel and allow to stand for 5 minutes (this creates steam and releases the potatoes from the bottom of the pan). Turn the potatoes over, pour over enough hot stock to just cover the potatoes, add the thyme and bring to the boil. Reduce down until the liquid has virtually evaporated and the potatoes are soft but still hold their shape. Remove them from the pan and keep warm.

Trim the asparagus and blanch in boiling, salted water for 1 minute, refresh in ice-cold water to keep the colour and pat dry on kitchen paper. Cut the Parma ham into long strips about 1.5cm wide and wrap a slice of ham around each asparagus spear.

Wipe the mushrooms clean with a damp cloth. If they're small keep whole, just cut off the end of the stalk, if they're large, cut into small pieces. Place the mushrooms into a very hot pan with a little olive oil and sauté for about 3 minutes. Drain in a colander.

Sweat the shallots and garlic in a little oil for a few minutes, add the mushrooms and cook for another couple of minutes, season with salt and pepper and finish with chopped parsley. Keep warm. Season the trout and lightly pan-fry over a low heat with a little oil until lightly golden. Then transfer the fish to a preheated oven at 190ºC for about 5 minutes. Pan-fry the asparagus with a little oil until the Parma ham is lightly golden.

For the dressing, squeeze the lemon juice into a bowl, add the mustard and whisk in the horseradish, then add the vegetable oil and olive oil and carry on whisking, season and stir in the tarragon. Leave to one side for a couple of minutes. To serve, put a helping of potatoes at the top of the plate, below that place a helping of mushroom and put a trout fillet on top. Lean the asparagus around the trout and pour some dressing around the outer edge of the plate.

Cold Poached Salmon with a Dill and Chive Potato Salad with Celeriac Crisps and Kent Asparagus

ingredients

Serves 4

4 supremes of salmon weighing
    about 225g each, pinboned and
    descaled
4 medium potatoes, peeled and
    diced into 1cm cubes
1 litre vegetable oil
16 asparagus spears
a few fronds of dill and half a
    bunch of chives
half a celeriac
half a portion of vinaigrette
    (see recipe page 198)
3 pints court bouillon
    (see recipe page 187)
about 2 tbsp of mayonnaise
salt and pepper

Bring the court bouillon to the boil and allow to simmer for 5 minutes. Season the salmon lightly, put into the court bouillon, allow to come back to the boil and then turn off the heat so the salmon cools in the liquid. Cook the potatoes in lightly salted water until just cooked and tender. It is important that the potatoes are cut into even pieces as this ensures even cooking. Drain the potatoes, put them in a bowl and pour over enough vinaigrette to coat them evenly. Let the potatoes cool naturally and they will absorb all the lovely flavour of the vinaigrette. When the potatoes are cool, add the chopped dill, the chives and mayonnaise, season if necessary and mix together, taking care not to break up the potatoes.

Peel the asparagus and blanch in boiling water for 1 minute. Immediately place in cold water to refresh and to keep the colour. Peel and shape the celeriac into a nice big round so you can slice finely into even rounds. Heat the vegetable oil to 170°C if you have a fryer (if not use a large pan). Put the celeriac slices into the oil a few at a time to fry until crisp and golden. Be careful – the moisture in the celeriac may make the fat spit a little. Drain the celeriac crisps on kitchen paper and season with salt while still hot.

To serve, place the potato salad in the centre of the plate, put a piece of salmon on top, sprinkle over a little sea salt and a few drops of olive oil. Put the celeriac crisps on top of this, roll the asparagus in a little vinaigrette, cut in half and surround the salmon with the spears.

Fish Recipes from Another Age

From *Good Things in England: A Practical Cookery Book for Everyday Use*, containing traditional and regional recipes suited to modern tastes – edited by Florence White ('Mary Evelyn'), founder of the English Folk Cookery Association. Published by the Cookery Book Club by arrangement with Jonathan Cape in 1968

to bake a codling: recipe 1777

1. Draw a codling, wash it well and dry it.
2. Take some oysters, some sweet herbs chopped small, some grated bread.
3. Mix these ingredients together, and use them to stuff the codling.
4. Lay it in a baking dish on a rack to keep it from hitting the bottom.
5. Put into the dish some red wine.
6. Baste the codling well with butter before it is put into the oven.
7. When it is done pour off the liquor which is under the codling into a saucepan, with a piece of butter rolled in flour.
8. Let these boil together till of a proper thickness.
9. Add some shrimps or oysters and a little anchovy to give flavour.
10. Heat up and serve.

N. B. The codling lies best in the dish with its tail turned in its mouth. Bass may be cooked in the same manner. A small salmon or trout is good baked in this manner. (An epicure of the old school always insisted upon having his cod or codling rubbed all over with salt, placed in a dish in the larder, and kept there for at least 2 hours before cooking. The salt must be washed off before it is cooked. This method makes the flesh firmer.)

baked white fish, bacon and green peas: a lancashire recipe

Sea bream, fresh haddocks, rock salmon, codlings, fillets etc can all be

made into a savoury nourishing dish if cleaned and put into a brown baking dish, floured and covered with rashers of bacon (or some bread-crumbs or bits of butter or clarified beef dripping may be sprinkled over the fish, and the rashers of bacon can be rolled and placed along each side.) The dish is then baked in a good oven and will be done in about half an hour. Bacon with fish is a favourite dish with fisher-folk, and at Blackpool green peas are always served with it.

an eighteenth-century cod stew

1. Take a pound of large cod, and the sounds (which must be blanched and if dried they must be boiled until tender), also the roe (blanched and washed clean) and the liver.
2. Cut the latter in round pieces.
3. Put them all into a stewpan, the large pieces of cod in the middle with a bunch of sweet herbs, a quarter of a pint of broth or boiling water, and half a pint of white wine.
4. Add some ground mace, an onion, some grated nutmeg, and some salt.
5. Cover them close, let them stew 5 or 6 minutes.
6. Then put in a dozen oysters with their liquor strained, and a piece of butter rolled in flour.

7. Shake the pan round till they are enough, and the sauce of a good thickness.
8. Take out the sweet herbs and onion.
9. Lay the fish in a dish and pour the sauce over it.

minnow tansies: a seventeenth-century recipe

Ingredients:
Minnows;
Yolks of eggs;
Cowslip 'pips' (or flowers) or
primrose petals;
A very little tansy juice;
And a little clarified fat in which
to fry them.

Wash the minnows well in salt, cut off their heads, tail them and take out their guts. Blend them with a few cowslip 'pips' or primrose petals, some yolks of egg and a very little tansy juice. Season with salt and pepper and fry them in a little fat as you would any other fritter.

Florence White, who wrote under the name of Mary Evelyn in the 1920s and 30s, came from a family of Sussex innkeepers. She was a great collector of recipes – many dating back hundreds of years – and some of which we've included here. She had a passion for cooking – English cooking – and the famous cookery writer Elizabeth David was a great fan. Miss White herself wrote in the introduction: 'This book is an attempt to capture the charm of England's cookery before it is completely crushed out of existence.' She especially liked weird and wonderful recipes dating back hundreds of years, which today we might find distasteful, such as one from the fifteenth century entitled 'How To Cook A Young Swan'. Others, which can still be useful today, include Salmagundy, 'a delightful and useful eighteenth-century salad'. This one – Salmagundy Without Meat – is suitable for a middle dish at supper or a good, light lunch. You serve it more or less like Spanish tapas, with plenty of bread.

1. In the top plate in the middle, which should stand higher than the rest, take a fine pickled herring, bone it, take off the head, mince the rest fine.

2.In the other plates around, put the following things: in one, pare a cucumber and cut it very thin; in another apples pared and cut small; in another an onion peeled and cut small; in another two hard eggs chopped small, the whites in one, the yolks in another; in another pickled gherkins cut small; in another celery cut small; in another pickled red cabbage chopped fine. Take some watercress; clean, washed and picked; stick them all about and between every plate and saucer and

throw nasturtium flowers about the cress. You must have oil and vinegar and lemon to eat with it.

If it is neatly set out it will make a pretty figure in the middle of the table or you may lay them in heaps in a dish.

Miss White, who founded The English Folk Cookery Association, died in 1940 and, sadly, the Association died with her.

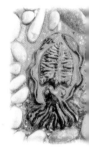

CHAPTER 8

Oily Fish

Everyone knows that oily fish is good for us – all those healthy oils – but many people would rather buy the fish-oil goodness in a capsule than try cooking the real thing. This is a shame because fish like mackerel, herring and sprats make wonderful meals.

Mackerel are not the most intelligent of fish and they're probably among the easiest to catch even though they are fast swimmers. Go out in a dinghy with a line of bait or even some twists of silvery paper like foil – they're attracted by the shimmering light – and you should bring in a good few meals. The meat of the mackerel is very rich and a little goes a long way. These are a very oily fish so remember they don't need oil when cooking. Simply clean and gut them, make a few cuts in their pretty greeny/brown skin to allow some of the oil to leave during cooking, sprinkle over some sea salt to crisp the skin and bake in the oven for about 10 minutes or so depending on the size of the fish. Like their posher neighbour, the bass, they're very versatile – you can bake them, grill them, they're wonderful thrown on the barbecue and they go well with crusty bread and mustard on the side. You can stuff them before you bake them – mackerel with apple is a perfect marriage and an apple-based stuffing with orange or lemon juice and a drop of wine works well in the oven. Experiment.

They are also delicious pickled, which is easier than it sounds. This works well with herring, too. First you need to make the souse – take a small piece of root ginger and give it a good bash to release the flavour to the full, dice a couple of chillis, add a few white and black peppercorns and mustard seeds – preferably black and yellow if you've got them. Now put some malt vinegar and water in a pan. Half and half is usually a good idea first time round but it's up to you – the more vinegar, the stronger the taste. If you want a sweet and sour taste add a pinch of sugar. Prepare your mackerel by gutting and cleaning,

the oyster seekers

descale if you want to (usually not necessary with mackerel but a good idea with herring) and trim the tail if you want them to look neater. Then put some of your spice mix on the bottom of a dish and lay the fish, top to tail, over it. Bring the vinegar to the boil, pour the hot vinegar over the fish and bake in the oven for about 15 to 20 minutes to half an hour. You can leave them to cool and eat them cold, or they are quite special eaten hot – the lovely, hot, spicy flavours get right up your nose – in the right way.

Herring are delicious grilled. Make a few cuts in the skin either side, sprinkle with a little salt and they only need to be cooked for about 3 or 4 minutes on each side. Be careful if the herring is carrying roe, the roe may take a little longer to do, so cook the fish, put aside to keep warm, take out the roe and give it a couple of extra minutes under the grill. One of Delia's favourite things is to eat the grilled herring and roe with mashed potato sprinkled with grated parmesan or stale dry mature cheddar cheese which has been flashed under the grill.

A rollmop is just a raw herring fillet which has been marinated in the same spices as the soused mackerel, but with white vinegar. It's easy to make your own – instead of baking the fish with the vinegar in the oven, pack the cleaned fillets into jars, add raw sliced onion and the spices and pour over the hot vinegar. They should be ready to eat within days and will keep well for a couple of weeks in their jar in the fridge.

Whitebait are the fry of herrings or mackerel and **sprats** are a kind of second division herring. In many restaurants they are dusted with flour and cayenne before being deep-fried. They're just as tasty if you don't have a deep-fryer or want to keep the calories down. Simply take a heavy frying pan, warm it on the hob, throw in some sea salt and then the fish. Keep shaking the pan while they cook in their own oil and add some more sea salt if you like. After just a few minutes serve them in a dish, perhaps on paper to absorb the extra oil. Add lemon wedges, salt and pepper, and some crusty bread.

Sardines are much nicer fresh than in tins and, like mackerel, they're wonderful fish for the barbeque. Although they're bigger than whitebait or sprats they are still especially good eaten in the fingers: hold them like you would a corn on the cob and munch along the bone. You will, of course, end up with very fishy fingers but in Portugal, where they are an everyday favourite, they've found the answer. If you can bring yourself to do it, pour some of your red wine into your hands – the Portuguese usually drink red wine with sardines – and rub your hands together. The fish smell miraculously goes. We don't get many sardines off the Kent coast – they like warmer water – so they're usually imported from Spain, but with our climate seeming to heat up each summer, local sardines might soon be as plentiful here as in the beach-bars of the Mediterranean.

Opposite: **The atmosphere at Wheelers is often chaotic, but somehow relaxing at the same time.**

the oyster seekers

Sardine Bruschetta

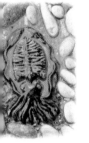

ingredients

Serves 4

1kg vine plum tomatoes,
    blanched, peeled, deseeded
    and petalled (i.e. quartered)
1 banana shallot, peeled and
    finely diced
4 slices of good, white bread
    (e.g. sour dough bread)
1 clove garlic, peeled
50g baby spinach
4 whole sardines, heads and fins
    removed, and gutted
few leaves of mint and basil
1 bay leaf
salt and pepper

First make the tomato compote. Sweat the shallots and some garlic in a pan for a few minutes. Do not allow the mixture to colour at all. Add the bay leaf, tomato petals, salt and pepper and allow to cook for about an hour, until all the tomato petals have broken down. Just before you finish cooking the tomato mixture, add some torn basil leaves and some torn mint leaves. Adjust seasoning and add a splash of olive oil.

Cut the garlic clove in half. Rub each slice of the bread with the garlic and then lightly toast the bread under the grill. The effect that you want is for the bread to have that lovely charred flavour.

Take a non-stick frying pan and dry-fry the sardines with a little sea salt. Place the slices of bread on a plate and top with the baby spinach leaves. Add a spoonful of the tomato compote and then the sardines. Serve with a small rocket salad.

Spicy Soft Herring Roes with Pieces of Pancetta Served with Hot Buttered Toast

ingredients

Serves 4

125g pancetta
350g herring roes
4 slices of toast
lemon juice
a pinch of cayenne, a pinch of
    curry powder and a little plain
    flour to coat the roes

Cut the pancetta into ½cm slices, cut away the rind leaving a little of the fat, then cut into even-sized batons. Fry in a pan over a low heat and allow to go crispy; remove the bacon and drain, leaving the fat in the pan. Add the cayenne and curry powder to the flour and sieve into a clean bowl.

Lightly season the herring roes with salt, put into the flour mix and lightly dust. Shake off any excess flour and fry the herring roes in the bacon fat quickly until golden. Toast the bread, remove the crusts, add the bacon bits to the herring roes. Put the herring roes on the toast, finish with a squeeze of lemon juice or sprinkle over a few capers.

the oyster seekers

Devilled Whitebait

ingredients

Serves 4

500g whitebait
200ml milk
8 slices of good brown bread,
 buttered
vegetable oil to fry with
50g softened butter
a good pinch of cayenne, salt
 and lime wedges to serve

Use fresh whitebait if you can, but frozen are almost as good. If using frozen, take them out of the freezer and allow to defrost naturally at room temperature. Sort through the whitebait when you wash them – being so small they can easily break. Discard these. After washing, drain on some kitchen paper.

Sieve the flour with the salt and cayenne. Drop the whitebait into the milk a few at a time and then into the flour evenly coating the fish. Then sieve the fish over a clean bowl to get rid of any excess flour. Now cook the whitebait in hot oil – if you have a fryer it should be at 200ºC, if not you can use a large pan of oil – but be careful! – and cook until they're golden and crispy.

The secret of successful whitebait is not to cook too many at one time, so, depending on how many you're serving, cook them in batches. Serve with the buttered brown bread and lime wedges.

Oatmeal-Coated Sprats Served with a Salad of Saffron Potatoes, Mustard Seeds and Crispy Pancetta

ingredients

Serves 4

6 sprats per person, gutted
   and heads removed
600g new potatoes, scrubbed
   or peeled
2½ pints of chicken stock
a good pinch of saffron strands
   (these stamens from the crocus
   are expensive but you need very
   few, so one jar lasts)
25g mustard seeds
some mixed salad leaves
one portion of basic vinaigrette
   (see recipe page 198)
a few sprigs of chervil and a few
   batons of chives
8 slices of pancetta, sliced thinly
oatmeal
butter and four wedges of lemon
2 tsp chopped parsley

Add the saffron strands to the stock and bring to the boil, then allow to cool. Peel or scrub the new potatoes, put them in the saffron stock, bring to the boil and simmer until just cooked. Remove the potatoes from the stock and allow to cool.

Cut the pancetta into lardons and grill until golden and crispy. Remove the lardons and allow to drain on some kitchen paper. Put the mustard seeds in a hot pan until they start to pop. Mix the cooked mustard seeds with the potatoes.

Pick over the salad leaves, add the chervil and the chives and leave in the fridge for the time being. Break two eggs into a bowl and lightly whisk. Put the oatmeal into a separate bowl.

Put a pan on the heat with some olive oil. When the oil is hot, dip the sprats first into the egg, then into the oatmeal, then fry them in the pan. Do the fish in batches. You might occasionally have to add a knob of butter to allow the fish to cook through. Move the fish around in the pan so that they're evenly cooked.

Rewarm the potatoes, add the parsley to the potatoes and lightly toss the salad in some vinaigrette. To serve, put the potatoes on the plate, with the oatmeal sprats and the salad. Sprinkle with crispy pancetta.

the oyster seekers

the oyster seekers

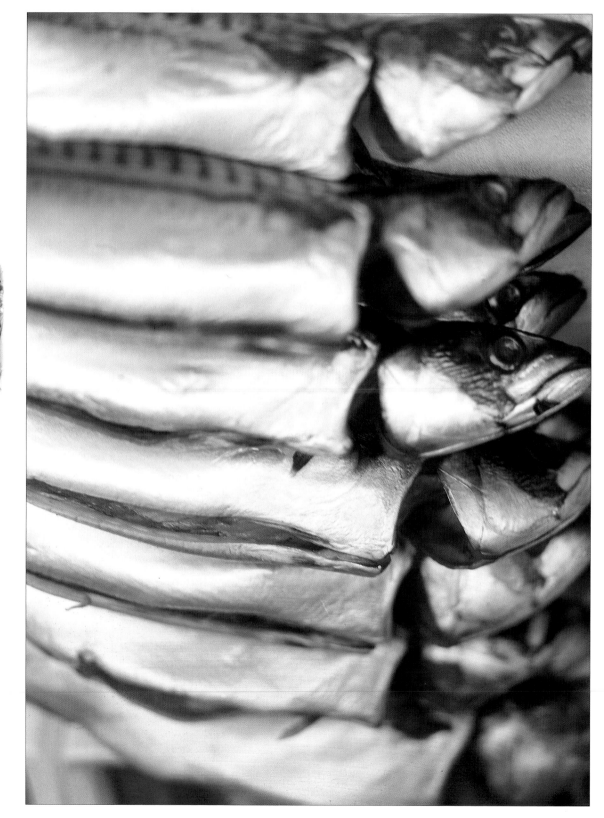

Grilled Mackerel on Braised Fennel with Coriander, Diced Tomato Served with a Sweet Mustard Beurre Blanc

ingredients

Serves 4

4 whole mackerel weighing about 225g each after the guts and head have been removed

2 bulbs of fennel

3 plum tomatoes, blanched, peeled, deseeded and evenly diced

750ml vegetable stock

250ml Pernod

50ml white wine

2 star anise

10 coriander seeds

50ml double cream

225g unsalted butter

2 cloves garlic

a few sprigs of thyme, a little fresh coriander, juice of one lemon, a pinch of cayenne

2 tbsp of Savora sweet mustard

Make three cuts across the body of each mackerel and put the fish in a baking tray. Put the lemon thyme with the garlic and a little olive oil in a pestle and mortar and lightly grind together. Rub this mixture into the cuts in the mackerel, pour over a little more olive oil, cover with clingfilm and put in the fridge for about 2 hours.

Remove the fennel stalks; peel, get rid of any tough strands and cut the bulb in half. Bring the vegetable stock, Pernod, wine, star anise and coriander seeds to the boil. Add the fennel and simmer for 5 minutes until the it is tender. Remove with a slotted spoon, then boil to reduce the sauce to about 100ml. Add the cream, bring to the boil, remove from the heat and allow to cool slightly. Cube the butter and whisk the cubes, gradually, into the sauce, until it thickens enough to coat a spoon. Whisk in the mustard, add a bit of lemon juice and season. Remove the core from the cooked fennel and slice evenly lengthways.

Put a little butter and a little water into a pan over a gentle heat and allow to emulsify, add the fennel, the fresh coriander, the tomato dice and season. When it's all well mixed together, take off the heat, season and keep warm. Now take the mackerel out of the fridge, season lightly inside and out, squeeze over a little lemon juice and grill for 5 minutes on each side. To serve, put the fennel in the centre of the plate, put the cooked mackerel on top, pour a little beurre blanc around the edges and serve with some creamy mashed potatoes.

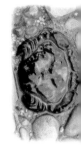

CHAPTER 9

Pies, Tarts and Flans

F
ish flans, pies, tarts and tortes are a good freezer standby and also make a perfect light lunch or supper served warm or cold, with a good mixed salad. To make the dishes in this chapter, you can use puff or shortcrust pastry (see recipes on pages 194 and 195). Although shop-bought will do, the end result will be much better if you make your own.

Choose firm fish, like haddock or tuna and salmon. Prawns and lobster work well too. The secret to making these kinds of dishes is to bake the pastry case first and allow it to cool completely, before adding the filling and then cooking it to finish. Although most will freeze, as many are egg-based, they shouldn't be kept in the fridge for longer than a couple of days. Don't be tempted to heat them in the microwave – they'll splatter everywhere. Always use the oven.

The tarts, flans and pies in this chapter are designed to serve between four and six people, but how many they feed will rather depend on the appetites of those you are cooking for!

Smoked Trout and Leek Tart Finished with Crème Fraiche and Horseradish Filling

ingredients

half portion of shortcrust pastry
   (see recipe page 194)
150g smoked trout fillet
the white of one leek, diced
200g crème fraiche
125ml double cream
squeeze of lemon juice
4 tsp horseradish sauce
1 egg and 1 egg yolk
a pinch of cayenne, salt and
   pepper and a few chopped
   chives

Roll out the pastry until about ½cm thick and line an 8-inch flan dish, then bake blind in a preheated oven at 180ºC until golden brown and cooked. Allow to cool. Sweat the leeks in a little oil for a few minutes, spread out on to a tray or plate, and allow to cool a little. In a bowl, mix the crème fraiche, double cream, horseradish, lemon juice, cayenne, salt and chives. Mix well. Whisk the egg and egg yolk together and fold into the crème fraiche. Put the leeks on the pastry base, then break the trout into even pieces and distribute evenly on top. Pour over the crème fraiche mix and allow to settle for a couple of minutes. Bake in a preheated oven at 190ºC for about 15 minutes until set. If the tart hasn't glazed – if it isn't nice and golden brown – quickly pop it under the grill for a minute or two, then allow it to cool for 10 minutes. Serve warm with a crisp, green salad.

A Torte of Fresh Lobster Infused with Tarragon

ingredients

2 lobsters, approx 450g each
half a leek
1 carrot
a quarter of a celeriac
1 medium shallot
10 Shitake mushrooms
250g puff pastry (see recipe page 195)
75ml cream
2 egg yolks, beaten
a pinch of cayenne, a few sprigs of tarragon and the juice of half a lime
4 large ramekins and flour for dusting

Roll out the pastry to about 2mm thick. Lightly dust the ramekins with flour, then line them with the pastry allowing some of the pastry to hang over the edge of each ramekin. Put in the fridge to rest for 15 minutes.

Blanch the lobster in boiling water for 1 minute then plunge into cold water to stop the cooking process. Prepare the lobster according to the diagram on page 82. Remove the meat from the lobster and remove the back trail.

Finely dice the shallot, leek, carrot, celeriac and mushrooms (this is called a fine 'dice brunoise' in the trade). Sweat the shallots in a little butter for a few minutes, add the leeks, and cook for another couple of minutes. Then add the carrot, celeriac and mushroom, and cook for 2 more minutes. Season with salt and add the cayenne. Add the cream, turning up the heat so the sauce reduces a little. Stir well, cook for about 3 minutes, then add the lime juice. Chop the tarragon finely and mix into the sauce, pour the ragout on to a tray and allow to go cold.

Slice the lobster into even-sized pieces, remove the pastried ramekins from the fridge and divide the lobster pieces between them. Add a little vegetable mix to each; then more lobster; then more vegetable mix, layering to the top; finish with a layer of vegetable mix. Fold over the excess pastry and seal each torte, then carefully invert the ramekins on a greased baking tray and remove the dishes. Brush the pastry cases with the egg mix, and bake at 230ºC for about 15 to 20 minutes until golden brown. Serve with a good crisp salad of mixed leaves. A truffle vinaigrette works well with this dish.

Opposite: **There are still only four tables in the back parlour at Wheelers.**

Salmon, Asparagus and Red Pesto Tart

ingredients

225g fresh salmon
250g shortcrust or puff pastry
6 asparagus spears
250ml crème fraiche
50ml double cream
2 tsp red pesto
1 whole egg and 1 egg yolk
a pinch of salt, a pinch of cayenne
and a little lemon juice

Roll out the pastry to about 2mm thick and line an 8-inch pastry tin. Bake blind in the oven at 220ºC for about 15 minutes, until the pastry is cooked and golden. Remove the skin from the salmon, evenly slice, then cover with clingfilm and put in the fridge. Trim the asparagus, blanch in boiling salted water for a minute, then refresh in cold water to keep the colour.

In a bowl, mix the crème fraiche, cream, red pesto, egg yolk, egg, salt and cayenne. Taste and check the seasoning.

Put the salmon pieces evenly around the bottom of the pastry base, put the asparagus spears on top evenly spaced like the hands of a clock, pour over the crème fraiche mix. Allow the mixture to settle for 5 minutes, then put on a baking tray and bake at 190ºC for about 15 minutes until set. Serve hot or cold with a green salad.

Smoked Haddock Flan

ingredients

1 portion of shortcrust pastry –
in this case you really must
make your own mixed with
sesame seeds and a little finely
chopped rosemary.

½ pt milk

300g undyed smoked haddock

1 portion bechamel sauce
(see recipe page 191)

1 shallot, finely diced

1 garlic clove, finely diced

4 plum tomatoes

1 courgette

5 button mushrooms

1 tsp Dijon mustard

1 tsp chopped parsley, ½ tsp
Worcester sauce, 8
peppercorns, 1 bay leaf, salt,
pepper and a little
grated cheddar cheese to
sprinkle on top of the flan

Line an 8-inch pastry case with the pastry – if you're making your own according to our recipe, add the sesame seeds and rosemary halfway through making the pastry, just before you add the eggs and water.

To cook the haddock, bring the milk to the boil with the bay leaf and peppercorns, add the haddock, then remove from the heat and allow to go cold. Blanch, peel and deseed the tomatoes and cut into even dice. Dice the courgettes and slice the mushrooms.

Sweat the shallot with the garlic in a little oil over a gentle heat for a couple of minutes, add the courgettes and cook for another couple of minutes, then do the same with the mushrooms and tomatoes. Stir well and season, take off the heat and allow to cool, then spread the mixture evenly over the pastry base. Take the haddock out of the milk – reserving the milk – and flake the haddock over the vegetable ragout mixture.

Make the bechamel sauce using the haddock milk. Finish the sauce with a teaspoon of Dijon mustard, the Worcester sauce, chopped parsley and a little seasoning. Spoon the sauce over the haddock, sprinkle with the grated cheese and glaze in the oven at 190ºC until golden brown.

the oyster seekers

Glazed Crab and Prawn Tartlets with Poppy Seed Shortcrust Pastry

ingredients

half a portion of shortcrust pastry
(see recipe page 194) mixed
with a few poppy seeds
1 portion hollandaise sauce
(see recipe page 193)
226g white crabmeat
450g whole prawns
1 tsp chopped parsley and a few
sprigs of chervil, snipped with
scissors
8 tartlet cases or tins
baking beans

You can cook your own crab and reserve the brown meat for another recipe (or have it on hot buttered toast). Alternatively, you can buy the white crabmeat from your fishmonger. Roll out the pastry until it's quite thin, then line the tart cases with it. Line with greaseproof paper, fill each with baking beans then bake blind in a preheated oven at 190ºC for about 15 minutes.

Remove the baking beans and the greaseproof paper and allow to cool on a wire rack. While the pastry is cooling, peel the prawns. You can use ready peeled, but the shells-on prawns which you peel yourself really do taste better.

Make the hollandaise sauce and add the parsley and snipped chervil. Divide the crab and prawns evenly between the tartlet cases, spoon over the hollandaise and glaze under a hot grill until golden brown. Serve with a crisp salad dressed with vinaigrette.

the oyster seekers

Soups, Sauces, Oils . . . and More

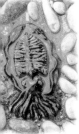

G ood, fresh fish served plain is delicious, but some fish take wonderfully well to sauces, as long as you remember that you should never make a sauce so strong that it overpowers and detracts from the flavour of the fish. We regularly make and sell large batches of fresh fish stock, which is a great standby. Use fresh, or it freezes well.

Fish Soup

ingredients

1 tsp tomato purée
1 medium fennel bulb, roughly
    chopped
2 leeks, the whites roughly
    chopped
1 medium onion, chopped
1 medium carrot, roughly chopped
2 cloves garlic
6 plum tomatoes, skinned,
    deseeded and chopped
a quarter of a celeriac, roughly
    chopped
250ml extra virgin olive oil
100ml Cognac
250ml dry white wine
100ml Ricard
mixed fish: 2 red mullet, 2 John
    Dory, 2 plaice, 1 monk tail (you
    can use just about any fish you
    like but avoid oily fish, which
    will make your soup
    unpleasantly greasy)
pinch of saffron
3 star anise
10 coriander seeds
10 black peppercorns
bouquet garni of parsley stalks,
    bay leaf, lemon thyme
sea salt and fresh pepper plus a
    little cayenne
juice of half a lemon

Scale and gut the fish, removing the head and fins. Cut into even-sized pieces – you do not have to remove the bones. Wash the fish, removing any excess debris, and allow to drain.

Put all the chopped vegetables into a roasting tray except the tomatoes and tomato purée. Pour over about 150ml of the olive oil and toss lightly so the vegetables are evenly coated. Sprinkle with a little sea salt, the coriander seeds, black peppercorns, star anise and a pinch of saffron. Mix thoroughly. Put in a preheated oven at 180ºC and allow them to slowly caramelise and roast. When the vegetables are cooked, put them in a stockpot or big saucepan, add the tomato purée and tomatoes and cook over a low heat for another 5 minutes.

While that's going on, pan-fry the fish pieces quickly in a hot pan, flambé with the brandy (igniting the brandy cooks out the alcohol) then, when the flames have gone, add the fish to the vegetables. Now add the Ricard and white wine and cook until the liquid is reduced to virtually nothing. Cover all this with fish stock and bring to the boil. Skim away any scum that comes to the surface and turn down so it's barely simmering. Cook for about 35 minutes and then add the bouquet garni. After another 15 minutes, remove the herbs and blitz the soup mix in small batches. Pass each batch through a fine sieve into a clean pan, using the back of a ladle to push it through. Discard any debris that won't go through the sieve. Bring the soup back to the boil, check the seasoning and consistency – if it's too thick, add a little more stock. Finish by whisking in a little cayenne and some freshly squeezed lemon juice. The soup freezes well.

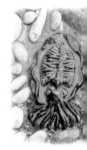

Whitstable Oysters Wrapped in Pancetta Served in a Leek and Potato Soup

ingredients

Serves 4

2 medium leeks, finely diced
1 large onion, finely diced
1 large potato, evenly diced
   (make the dice quite small)
850ml chicken stock
   (see recipe page189)
12 Whitstable Rocky oysters
6 pieces finely sliced pancetta
165g butter
1 tsp chopped chives, salt and
   pepper

Finely dice the white and light green of the leeks but get rid of any tough dark green bits. Rinse well under cold water. Dice the onion and potato – keeping them separate.

Gently sweat the onions in the butter for a couple of minutes – don't let them brown – then add the leek and cook for a few more minutes before adding the potatoes with enough stock to cover. Bring to the boil and pour over the vegetables. Season with salt and pepper, and cook for about 10 minutes until the veg are cooked.

Blend the soup in a food processor or blender and pass through a sieve into a clean pan. Bring back to a simmer and check the seasoning and consistency.

Open the oysters, wrap each in half a thin slice of pancetta and cook under a hot grill for 1 minute. To serve, pour the soup into bowls, garnish with three wrapped oysters per bowl and sprinkle with fresh chives.

Fish Cream Sauce

ingredients

4 medium shallots, very
   finely diced
75g butter
200ml Noilly Prat
200ml dry white wine
6 whole white peppercorns
6 parsley stalks (use the green
   for garnish)
1 bay leaf
500ml fish stock
300ml double cream
200ml single cream
juice of half a lemon
pinch of cayenne and sea salt

Sweat the shallots in the butter until nice and soft but not brown then add the peppercorns and parsley stalks. While the shallots are cooking, put the stock in a separate pan and bring to a simmer (this allows you to reduce the cooking time of the sauce, keeping it as fresh as possible). Pour the white wine and Noilly Prat into the shallots, allow to come to the boil and allow to reduce by half. Now add the hot stock to the shallot pan, allow to come back to the boil and reduce down again by half.

While that's happening, mix the creams together in another pan and bring to the boil, immediately add to the shallot pan and simmer gently until the sauce coats the back of a spoon. Add a squeeze of lemon juice along with some seasoning of salt and cayenne. Taste, season if necessary and pass through a sieve. Use as required. This will keep in the fridge for two days.

Marinière Sauce

ingredients

one celery stick
2 onions
1 shallot
2 cloves of garlic
parsley
bay leaf
100ml white wine
350ml fish stock
knob of butter

Sweat the onions, shallot, celery, garlic and parsley sauce in a pan. Do not allow them to brown. Add the white wine, simmer and allow to reduce a little. Add the fish stock and the bay leaf, bring to the boil and simmer for five minutes. Remove the parsley stalks and the bay leaf, add a small knob of butter and serve.

Court Bouillon

ingredients

4 shallots, cut in half
3 large carrots
3 medium leeks
3 celery sticks
1 large fennel
1 stick lemon grass
3 star anise
20 coriander seeds
8 white peppercorns
200ml white wine vinegar
300ml dry white wine
3 litres water
a bouquet garni of lemon, thyme,
    tarragon and parsley stalks
pinch of sea salt
1 lemon, quartered

Cut all the vegetables into even-sized pieces and wash thoroughly. Put the vegetables with the bouquet garni into a pan, cover with water then add the white wine and vinegar. Bring to the boil. Add all the rest of the dry ingredients including a pinch of sea salt, return to the boil and simmer for 30 to 35 minutes. Once cooked, remove from the heat, add the lemon quarters and allow to cool. Once cool, pass through a sieve and use as required. Use as needed. This will last for about 4 days in a fridge or for up to 3 months in the freezer.

Wheelers Fish Stock

ingredients

2kg fish bones: brill, turbot, soles,
   halibut – avoid oily fish or your
   stock will be unpleasantly
   greasy
350ml white wine
560g button mushrooms
1150g unsalted butter
1 fennel
1 white of leek
1 onion
2 celery sticks
8 peppercorns
8 parsley stalks
1 lemon, cut into 4

Soak the fish bones in a bowl under a running cold tap removing any blood or blood clots. Drain, chop up and shake off any excess water. Chop the fennel, leek, celery and onion, and sweat in the butter until soft but not coloured. Add the fish bones, and allow to cook for another few minutes. Add the wine, and allow to cook out until almost dry without burning. Add cold water until you've just covered everything, add the parsley stalks and peppercorns, allow to come to the boil, reduce the heat immediately and simmer. Simmer for about 30 minutes, removing any scum that comes to the surface. Now put the stock into a clean pan, add the sliced mushrooms and lemon wedges, and allow to go cold. Once it is cold you should be left with a clear gelatinous stock. Either freeze the stock or keep in the fridge and use within three days.

White Chicken Stock

ingredients

1 large boiler chicken or 4kg
  chicken bones
5 carrots
3 leeks
2 medium onions
1 head of garlic
3 celery sticks
2 bay leaves
8 peppercorns
5 sprigs thyme
sea salt and 6 litres of water

Put the raw chicken or chicken bones into a stockpot or big pan, cover with the water, bring to the boil and simmer, skimming any scum that floats to the surface.

When the chicken has been boiled and skimmed add the vegetables and the herbs, making sure they're all submerged in the water. Allow the stock to come back to the boil and simmer for about 3 to 4 hours, depending on how strong you want the stock – the longer the cooking the stronger the taste. Taste as you go along. When cooked, strain the stock through a colander to remove the bones and vegetables, then sieve the stock into a clean bowl. Now you can freeze the stock and it will last for up to three months, or you can keep it for up to a week in the fridge as long as you bring it to the boil every couple of days during that time. When a stock has come to the boil never allow it to carry on boiling rapidly or it will go cloudy on you – the stock should be a lovely golden clear colour. Always allow stock to just simmer slowly.

the oyster seekers

Garlic Rouillé

ingredients

2 egg yolks
½ tsp tomato purée
pinch of saffron
1 medium chilli, finely diced
1 sweet red pepper
3 cloves of garlic, roughly
  chopped
1½ slices of fresh white bread
4 tbsp fish stock
pinch of paprika, salt, pepper
120ml olive oil
100ml peanut oil or vegetable oil
  (peanut is better)

Remove the crusts from the bread. Cut the bread into small pieces, pour over the fish stock and allow the bread to soak up the stock for a few minutes. Grill the sweet pepper until the skin blisters, then allow to cool. Skin, quarter, deseed and cut into small pieces. Remove the seeds from the chilli and finely dice.

Put the egg yolks in a food processor along with the garlic, chilli, red pepper, soggy bread, saffron and blend until smooth. Then slowly add the oil until you have the consistency of mayonnaise. Check the seasoning and consistency, add a pinch of paprika and a few drops of lemon juice. This will keep for 1 day in the fridge.

Mayonnaise

ingredients

5 egg yolks
2 tsp English or Dijon mustard,
  according to taste
2 dessertspoons white wine
  vinegar
salt, pepper and the juice of a
  quarter lemon wedge
450ml vegetable oil
1 tbsp water

Place the sugar and cold water in a pan and heat until the sugar dissolves. Allow to cool completely. Put the egg yolks, mustard, vinegar, salt, pepper and sugar/water mix into a bowl and whisk until well blended. Then slowly add the oil, whisking all the time until the oil is all mixed in. Add the juice of the lemon and carry on whisking. Check the seasoning and consistency. If it's too thick, whisk in a couple of teaspoons of hot water. Make on the day you're eating: fresh mayonnaise doesn't keep. You can, of course, do all this by hand, but using a food processor does make life easier.

Bechamel Sauce

ingredients

1 pint fresh whole milk
1 onion
2 cloves
1 bay leaf
52g unsalted butter
52g flour
1 tsp good English mustard
   and salt and pepper

Peel the onion, leave whole and pin the bay leaf to the onion with the cloves. Put the onion into the milk and bring to the boil. Immediately remove from the heat and allow to infuse for about 30 minutes. Pass the milk through a sieve into a clean jug. Gently melt the butter, sieve the flour into the butter and stir with a wooden spoon to form a roux. Cook for about 3 minutes. Slowly beat the milk into the roux, bit by bit, then, when all the milk is in, bring it to the boil and immediately back to simmer. Simmer very slowly for about 15 minutes (this allows all the floury taste to be cooked out). Finish the sauce with a teaspoon of English mustard, salt and pepper, and mix well. Pass the sauce through a sieve and then cover with greaseproof paper to prevent a skin forming on the top. Put in the fridge when cold.

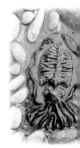

Shallot Vinegar

ingredients

1 vinegar jar or bottle
150ml red wine vinegar
1 medium shallot, very finely
   diced
8 Jamaican allspice seeds
pinch of salt

Place the vinegar, diced shallots and allspice into a pan, bring to the boil and remove from the heat immediately. Season with a little salt. Put into a clean vinegar jar and allow to stand at room temperature for 48 hours before use. What isn't used will last for up to a month, maturing in flavour. Store in the larder or fridge.

Hollandaise Sauce

ingredients

1 tbsp of reduction (see below)
250g butter
3 egg yolks
salt, cayenne pepper and a good
   squeeze of lemon

FOR THE REDUCTION :
1 litre white wine
10 crushed white peppercorns
8 coriander seeds
300ml white wine vinegar
15 parsley stalks
4 finely diced shallots

Make the reduction by placing all the ingredients in a pan, bring to the boil, then simmer until reduced by two-thirds. Allow to go cold, pass through a sieve and use what you need – the rest can be frozen or kept in the fridge for up to a week.

Allow the butter to melt in a pan and, once melted, remove any white solids that float to the top. Then strain the butter leaving the milky solids at the bottom of the pan. Put the egg yolks and 1 tablespoon of the reduction into a bowl. Place over a pan of just simmering water and whisk until the eggs start to thicken and go a lighter yellow. Remove from the pan, and slowly add the butter, whisking all the time until you've used up all the butter. Season the hollandaise with salt and cayenne pepper and a good squeeze of lemon juice. Keep covered and use the same day. Don't keep it in the fridge, as the butter will go hard.

the oyster seekers

Shortcrust Pastry

ingredients

225g plain flour
110g unsalted butter
1 egg yolk
pinch of salt
water

Sieve the flour and salt into a clean bowl. Dice the butter and rub into the flour until you have sandy breadcrumbs. Mix the egg yolk with 1 tablespoon of water, make a well in the centre of the flour, mix lightly to create a ball of pastry. Wrap in clingfilm and allow to rest in the fridge for 30 minutes before use.

Suet Pastry

ingredients

225g plain flour
13g baking powder
100g suet
150ml water
pinch of salt

Sieve the flour with the baking powder and salt – this distributes the ingredients and adds some air. Add the suet and evenly mix throughout the flour, Make a well in the centre of the mix, then add the water and mix together creating a fairly stiff paste. Wrap in clingfilm and put in the fridge for 30 minutes before using.

the oyster seekers

Puff Pastry

ingredients

450g plain flour
450g unsalted butter
300ml cold water
a good pinch of salt and a few
   drops of lemon juice

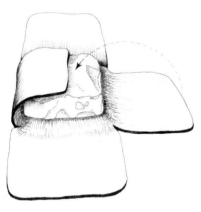

Making Puff Pastry

Remove 100g of the butter and set aside. Allow the rest of the butter to sit at room temperature for about 45 minutes.

Sieve the flour and salt together, then rub the 100g of butter into the flour until it looks like sandy breadcrumbs. Make a well in the centre of the flour. Mix the water and the lemon juice then slowly add the lemon water to the flour mix. Do this carefully, little by little, as you may not need it all, or you may need a little more. Bring the mixture to a smooth dough by kneading. Then wrap in clingfilm and allow to rest for 20 minutes.

Place the dough on a lightly floured surface. Cut a cross halfway down the dough and lightly pull out the corners. Now lightly roll out all the corners leaving a small mound in the middle of the dough, as per the diagram on the left. Mould your softened butter to the same shape as the mound. (The butter should be similar in texture to the dough itself – too soft and the butter will ooze out of the sides of the pastry, too hard and it will break through the paste.) Fold the dough corner flaps over the butter forming a rectangle, ensuring that all the butter is sealed in the dough. Allow to rest for 10 minutes.

Roll out the pastry until it's three times its original length, making sure no butter oozes out. Fold both ends of the pastry into the centre then fold over once more. Give the dough a quarter turn so the folded edge is either to your left or right. (This is known as a double turn.) Allow to rest for 20 minutes. Ideally you need to make three more turns, ensuring you rest the pastry for 20 minutes between turning. Wrap in clingfilm and allow to rest in the fridge until needed.

Coriander Pesto

ingredients

50g coriander leaves
20g roasted pine kernels
10g walnuts
1 clove garlic
5g salt
50g Parmesan
100ml virgin olive oil

Put the pine kernels, walnuts, garlic, Parmesan and salt in a food processor and blend. Add half the olive oil and blend again. With the motor still running, add the coriander leaves and then slowly add the rest of the oil. Continue blending until you have a creamy consistency, place in an airtight container and store in the fridge until needed. This pesto will not freeze.

Welsh Rarebit Mixture

We use Welsh rarebit with haddock and other recipes – and it does go wonderfully well with fish. This Gary Rhodes recipe is fantastic.

ingredients

350g mature Cheddar cheese, grated
85ml milk
25g plain flour
25g fresh white breadcrumbs
½ tbsp English mustard powder
a few dashes of Worcester sauce
1 egg plus 1 egg yolk
salt and pepper to season

Put the grated Cheddar and milk in a pan and melt the cheese slowly over a low heat. Don't allow the mixture to boil as this would allow the mix to separate. When the mixture just begins to bubble and is nice and smooth, add the flour, breadcrumbs and mustard and continue cooking over a low heat, stirring continuously. When the mixture starts to come away from the sides of the pan, remove from the heat. Add the Worcester sauce, salt and pepper, stir and leave to cool. When cold, put it in a food processor, turn on and slowly add the egg and egg yolk. Put into a bowl and use as required.

Herb Oil

ingredients

2 bunches of herbs, for example
   basil, chervil, chives, parsley
   and tarragon or any other
   preferred combination
100ml olive oil
salt to taste

Whatever herbs you choose you need to pick them over and discard any tough stalks. Blanch the herbs in boiling salted water for just 30 seconds. Remove immediately and plunge the herbs into ice-cold water. When they're cold, remove from the water, squeeze to remove any excess water, put into a food processor and blend, slowly adding the oil. Pass through muslin or a sieve into a clean bottle or jar, adding seasoning to taste. This oil will last for 2 days in the fridge without losing its colour.

the oyster seekers

Lemon and Vanilla Confit

ingredients

3 large lemons
150ml water
1 tsp caster sugar
1 vanilla pod, split and
    deseeded

Grate the zest from the lemons, being careful not to take off any of the bitter white pith – a lemon zester is really best for this. Juice all the lemons, sieve the juice, put into a pan with the zest, vanilla, sugar and water, bring to the boil and simmer until reduced by half and the sauce is lemony and syrupy. Pour into a clean airtight container, put in the fridge and use as required. This will keep for 1 week in the fridge – and you can use all those egg whites to make meringues.

Vinaigrette

ingredients

2 tbsp grainy mustard
1 tsp sugar
salt and pepper
100ml cider vinegar
300 ml olive oil
2 tsp chopped dill

Put the mustard into a bowl along with the salt and pepper and vinegar and whisk until evenly mixed. Gradually whisk in the olive oil and dill. If the dressing becomes too thick add a little hot water.

Truffle Vinaigrette

ingredients

100ml extra virgin olive oil
1 tsp Dijon mustard
30ml groundnut oil
30ml truffle oil – expensive but
    very strong, so you use
    a little in each dish
1 tbsp cider vinegar
salt and pepper to season

First, put the mustard in a bowl and season with salt and pepper, add the vinegar and whisk thoroughly. Carry on whisking and slowly add the olive oil, truffle oil and groundnut oil. When thoroughly whisked, put in an airtight container until needed. If you're feeling very extravagant you could add some finely chopped truffle, but it isn't essential. This vinaigrette will keep for one week.

Balsamic Vinaigrette

ingredients

2 tbsp balsamic vinegar
2 tbsp olive oil
2 tbsp groundnut oil
salt and pepper

Place the vinegar, salt and pepper in a bowl and whisk. Gradually whisk in the oils. Check seasoning and use as required.

The Soup Kitchen

Traditionally when the going gets tough, the needy islanders get eating – fish.

During the Second World War, chef Ambrose Heath, 'the famous culinary expert', published a useful book for war-workers called *There's Time For A Meal*, with recipes for dishes which were good for you and could be cooked in double-quick time. He was encouraging people to take the trouble to cook a meal rather than 'have recourse to the cold comfort of tinned foods'.

Fish, cheap and plentiful, figured heavily, and soup was a favourite. He said: 'In these days of stress and hurry we may not be able to follow the usual amenities, but remembering that even during an Air Raid a stockpot can be kept simmering it will always be possible to serve a bowl of good soup when the "All Clear" has sounded.'

The idea of an entire population leaving their stockpots bubbling, while they were away in the air raid shelters, is somewhat mind-boggling today. And the soups on offer, at a time when you had to make the best of what you'd got, doesn't sound too appetising either. But they were nutritious – and cheap.

With fish soups he recommended adding forcemeat balls to spice things up a little and one of these broths was Cod's Head Soup:

Fry two chopped onions until golden in a little margarine and add two dessert-spoonfuls of flour mixed with a teaspoon of curry powder. Blend and add the cod's head. Cover with water, add three sliced tomatoes, a bay leaf, a sprig or two of parsley and a little thyme, bring to the boil and simmer for two or three hours. When done, strain and season.

Other suggestions included sandwiches filled with cold, cooked fish, anchovy spread and a few drops of Worcester sauce; shrimps with scrambled eggs; sprats in every which way; herrings baked or grilled; mackerel cooked in milk; sardines; scallops; and this ultra-fast fish stew called Souchet of Sole:

Put four slip soles into a pan, cover them with cold water, add a little salt, pepper and chopped parsley and a slice of onion. Bring to the boil and stew very gently for 10 minutes. Remove the onion on serving this simple stew, which some like to eat with brown bread and butter.

the oyster seekers

the oyster seekers

the oyster seekers

the healthy bit

Everyone knows that fish is good for you.

'But few really understand why,' says TV health guru, and Wheelers regular, Michael van Straten. 'It's because all fish are an excellent source of protein and don't contain the saturated fats that are found in animal fats like butter, cream and meat, too much of which – say nutritionists – lead to all sorts of ills.

'Flat fish are virtually fat free, contain lots of vitamins and minerals, and are a valuable source of iodine. Many of us are low on iodine, which is essential for a healthy thyroid gland, which in turn is essential for good metabolism. Edible seaweed – or seamarsh plants like samphire – are choc-a-bloc with iodine, so if you can combine your seafood meal of flat fish with some samphire you will do yourself some good.

'Oily fish contains what all health experts consider to be positive fats – omega-3-fatty acids. These are essential for the development of the brain, so pregnant women particularly are encouraged to eat oily fish like salmon, sardines, mackerel etc. each week for the benefit of the unborn child – and their own health. A recent study of 5,500 pregnant women in Scandinavia found that women who ate two portions or more of oily fish per week were less likely to have premature births. Oily fish also reduces the risk of thrombosis because the omega-3-fatty acids are anti-inflammatory and improve the flow of blood, which lowers the risk of strokes and heart disease. They are a rich source of vitamin D and we need vitamin D to absorb calcium. This, in turn, reduces the risk of osteoporosis – brittling of the bones – which afflicts many elderly people, especially women. Of course, you can get your beneficial omega-3 shot from things like cod liver oil capsules, but why spend out at the pharmacy when you can get the same dose by enjoying a meal of fresh mackerel cooked to perfection on the barbecue?

'Crabs are rich in B vitamins, especially vitamin B6, which is excellent for women who suffer from PMS. Lobsters hold lots of vitamin B12 and are full of selenium which protects against prostate cancer in men and breast cancer in women. Prawns, too, are a good source of vitamin B12, and shellfish, such as winkles and cockles, are rich in iron. And, of course, shellfish are virtually fat free. People suffering from gout should avoid eating too much, though, as the acids, which are healthy for most, can aggravate the condition, as Henry VIII found to his cost.'

But, best of all, says Michael, are oysters.

'They're full of vitamins and minerals and they deserve their reputation as an aphrodisiac. It's all that zinc in each mouthful that does it – and, for men, zinc is necessary for the manufacture of healthy sperm. As for women, oysters may also act as an aphrodisiac but more because of the sensuous act of eating an oyster. For men and women the concentration of minerals gives an instant boost.'

So if you want a totally loving and productive meal, Michael recommends a dozen oysters each, served with wholemeal bread, lightly buttered (a little animal fat – not too much – and the wholemeal is good source of fibre), wine in moderation (for enjoyment), plus his own aphrodisiac salad: Lovers Treat.

Put some watercress in a bowl (the cress is full of iron and mustard oils, which are a sexual stimulant). Add some peeled avocado (lots of vitamin E) and pine nuts (also full of vitamin E, plus minerals). Toss lightly with a good French dressing.

Eat, enjoy – and retire.

(SALAD FROM *SUPER SALADS – HEALING SALADS FOR MIND, BODY AND SOUL*)

the oyster seekers

Pearls

Delia can remember seeing only one 'proper' pearl in all the oysters she's opened. It was found many years ago in one opened by her mother, Martha. But she has found numerous tiny seed pearls – sadly too small to do anything with. A pearl develops when a body foreign to the oyster, such as a piece of grit, gets lodged in the oyster shell. To protect itself, it immediately begins to build concentric layers of material, thereby giving birth to a pearl. It's tropical oysters that produce those irridescent, glowing pearls which are so valuable commercially, and the rare black pearl is the most valuable of them all. But, alas, you won't find them here – so if you're a pearl seeker, head south.

Wheelers
Menus

the oyster seekers

This section contains a small selection of some of our menus from over the last five years. They illustrate how we have developed our culinary skill with fish. The first few menus contain relatively simple dishes whereas the later ones show our dishes becoming more innovative and adventurous. We hope our combinations of flavours will inspire you and encourage you to experiment with fish in your cooking.

wheelers menu 1

STARTERS

Baked New Zealand Mussels Gratinated
with a Garlic, Cheese & Herb Crust

Roasted Scallops Served with a Warm
Bacon & Mushroom Salad

Caesar Salad with Poached Haddock & Egg

Home-Made Salmon Cakes Served with
A Light Herb Salad

Home-Cured Salmon Served with Lemon
& Brown Bread Topped with Salad

MAIN COURSES

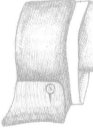

A Pave of Seared Salmon with Crushed New
Potatoes, Olives, Tomatoes & Herbs

Roast Cod with Baked Tomatoes and a
Balsamic Dressing

Fish Kebabs with a Lemon and Saffron Rice

Garlic Tiger Prawns with a Herb Rice

Bowl of Mixed Salad

Hot Potatoes

the oyster seekers

the oyster seekers

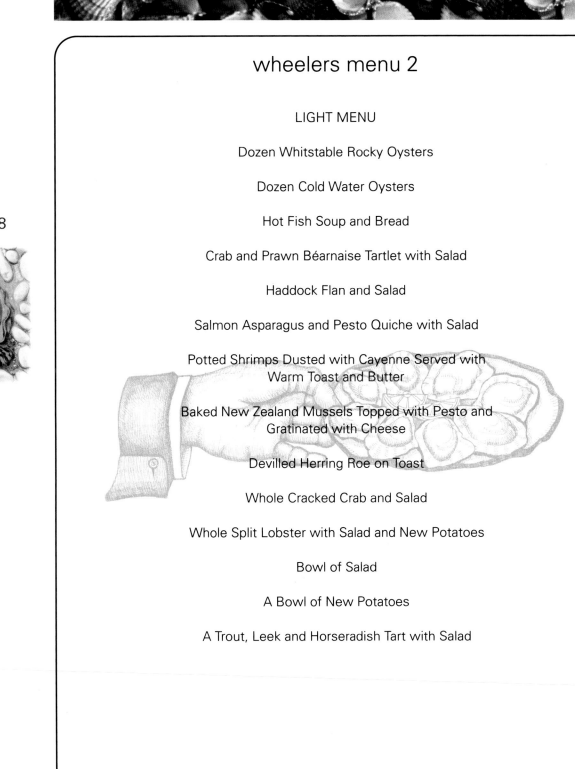

wheelers menu 2

LIGHT MENU

Dozen Whitstable Rocky Oysters

Dozen Cold Water Oysters

Hot Fish Soup and Bread

Crab and Prawn Béarnaise Tartlet with Salad

Haddock Flan and Salad

Salmon Asparagus and Pesto Quiche with Salad

Potted Shrimps Dusted with Cayenne Served with
Warm Toast and Butter

Baked New Zealand Mussels Topped with Pesto and
Gratinated with Cheese

Devilled Herring Roe on Toast

Whole Cracked Crab and Salad

Whole Split Lobster with Salad and New Potatoes

Bowl of Salad

A Bowl of New Potatoes

A Trout, Leek and Horseradish Tart with Salad

wheelers menu 2

COLD MENU

Mixed Seafood Platters

Whole Prawns and Bread

Bowl of Eels and Bread

Smoked Mackerel and Bread

Smoked Salmon with Lemon and Bread

King Prawns

Peeled Prawns

Winkles (when in season)

Crab Meat

Rollmops

Squid in Olive Oil and Peppers

Octopus in Olive Oil

Anchovies in Garlic Lemon Oil

Herring in Madeira

Herring in Sour Cream

Whole Baby Octopus

Whelks

Cockles

Mussels

the oyster seekers

wheelers menu 3

LIGHT MENU

Dozen Whitstable Rocky Oysters

Dozen Scottish Rocky Oysters

Dozen Whitstable Native Oysters (when in season)

Crab and Prawn Béarnaise Tartlet with Salad

Smoked Haddock and Cheese Flan with Salad

Salmon, Asparagus and Pesto Quiche with Salad

Trout, Leek and Horseradish Tart with Salad

Prawn and Dill Cocktail Served with Brown Bread and Butter

Toasted Bagels Spread with Cream Cheese and Chives
Layered with Scottish Smoked Salmon

Potted Shrimps dusted with Cayenne Served
with Warm Buttered Toast

Moules Marinière served with French Bread

Hot Fish Soup served with French Bread

Devilled Whitebait

Whole Cracked Crab with Salad

Whole Split Lobster with Salad and New Potatoes

Bowl of Salad

Bowl of New Potatoes

wheelers menu 3

COLD MENU

Mixed Seafood Platters

Whole Prawns and Bread

Bowl of Eels and Bread

Smoked Mackerel and Bread

Smoked Salmon with Lemon and Bread

King Prawns (each) with a Choice of Dip

Prawn Cocktail, Garlic or Plain Mayonnaise

Peeled Prawns with Lemon and Bread & Butter

Winkles (when in season)

Crab Meat with Lemon and Bread & Butter

Sweet or Sour Rollmops

Squid in Olive Oil and Peppers

Octopus in Olive Oil and Peppers

Whole Baby Octopus

Anchovies in Garlic Lemon Oil

Anchovies Wrapped Around Olives

Herring in Madeira

Herring in Dill Sauce

Herring in Mustard Sauce

Herring in Sour Cream

Crab Sticks

Whelks

Cockles

Mussels

the oyster seekers

wheelers menu 4

STARTERS

A Herb Imprinted Pasta of Smoked Haddock
and Spinach with Poached Quails Egg,
Chive and Grainy Mustard Buerre Blanc

A Terrine of Monkfish Set in a Cassoulet of
Cannellini Beans with Pancetta, Mixed Salad Leaves
and Warm Speciality Bread of the Day

An Envelope of Scottish Rope Grown Mussels
Steamed with White Wine, Lemon Thyme,
Lime Leaf and Coconut

A Tarte Fine of Fresh Crab Ginger and Coriander
with Wild Rocket and Fig Salad Surrounded by a
Honey and Citrus Dressing

Crispy Baby Squid and Roasted Queen Scallops
Served with Confit New Potatoes and a Salad of
Marinated Cucumber

Pan-Fried Crab Cake with a Pear, Celery,
Walnut and Rocket Salad

wheelers menu 4

MAIN COURSES

Grilled Whole Mackerel Served withFresh Piccalilli
and Creamy Pomme Purée

Sesame-Flecked Halibut on Baked Little Gems,
Butternut Squash, Samphire, Smoked Bacon
and Horseradish Veloute

Mustard-Coated Cod Served with a Glazed Baked
Rosemary Scented Onion, Wrapped in Parma Ham
with a Refreshing Chick Pea Salsa

Prawn and Scallop Brochettes Served
on a Mediterranean Linguine

Roast Monkfish Wrapped in Parma Ham
Served with Roast Pepper, Basil and Goats Cheese Pitivier

Pan-Fried John Dory on Lightly Crushed
Confit New Potatoes, Salad of Cannellini Beans with Fresh
Asparagus and New Season Pea & Mint Veloute

the oyster seekers

wheelers menu 5

STARTERS

Roasted Scallops Served with a Mixture of Bacon,
Mushrooms & Parmentier Potatoes

Moules Mariniere Served with French Bread

A Trio of Cured Salmon (Home-cured, Gravalax, & Scottish)
served with Freshly Baked Walnut Bread Accompanied by
Butter & Lemon. (Walnut Bread Saturdays only)

Home-Made Salmon Cakes Served with a
Light Herb Salad (Upon availability)

Hot Fish Soup Served with a French Stick

Pan-Fried Crab Cake Served with a Rocket
& Watercress Salad

The Freshest of Shellfish Folded into a Buttered Linguine and
Finished with a Light Cherry Tomato Sauce

Dozen Local Oysters Served in the Shell with a
Crispy Tempura and an Oriental Dipping Sauce

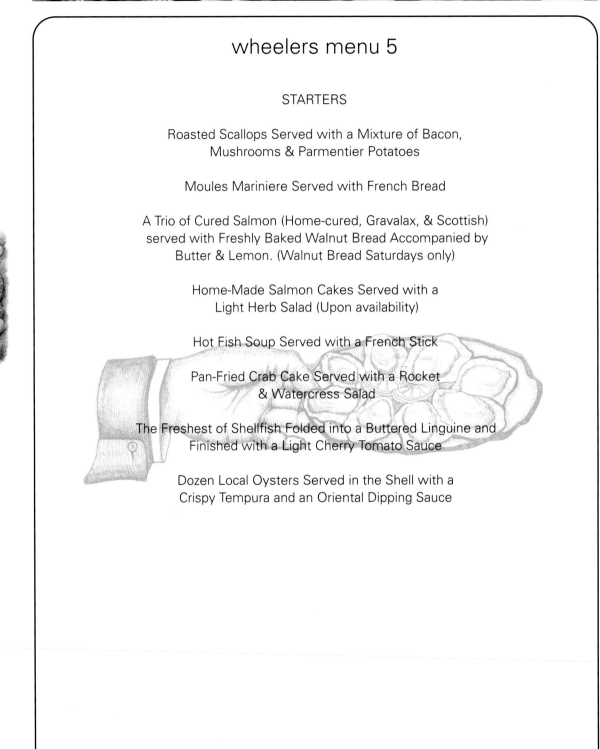

wheelers menu 5

MAIN COURSES

Roasted Salmon with Caramelized Chicory Wrapped in
Bacon Served with Tossed Swiss Chard Leaves & Drizzled
with a Dill & Sweet Mustard Vinaigrette

Local Home Smoked Haddock Topped with Welsh Rarebit Placed on a
Bubble & Squeak Cake Served with a Light Mustard Sauce

Coriander-Crusted Cod Placed Upon a Bed of Piperade Served
with a Rosti Potato & Crispy Pieces of Swiss Chard

Pan-Fried Sea Bass on a Bed of Braised Fennel, Tomato &
Saffron Served with a Creamy Garlic Mash

Baked Wings of Skate with a Green Peppercorn Crust Served with Pomme Dauphines,
Roasted Cherry Tomatoes Finished with a Bargoule Sauce

Grilled Tuna with a Creamy Horseradish Mash, French Beans
Tossed in Red Wine Vinegar and Coated with Creme Fraiche

Poached Smoked Local Haddock with a Poached Egg, Bubble and Squeak Fritters
and Drizzled with a Light Smokey Mustard Sauce

Roasted Cod Placed Upon Glazed Potatoes and Fresh Spinach
Served with a Crispy Parma Ham and a Parsley Sauce

Seared Salmon & Bois Boudin Sauce with Braised Lettuce & Roasted
Asparagus Accompanied by Home-Made Gnocci Potato

Baked Skate Rested on a creamy Leek Potato Garnished
with Roasted Seasonal Vegetables

Grilled Dover Sole Served with Parsley Buttered Potatoes Spinach, Asparagus
& Drizzled with a fresh Lemon Oil and Finished with Chives

Roasted Monkfish Accompanied by a Fondant Potato & Medley of Leeks, Tomatoes,
Olives & Parma Ham Served with a Fish Cream Sauce

the oyster seekers

wheelers menu 6

STARTERS

A Seafood Risotto Served with a Rocket & Cherry Tomato Salad
Topped with Parmesan & Oregano Crackling

Squid & Tiger Prawns Marinated in Lemon Grass, Lime Leaf & Coriander,
Accompanied with a Hot & Spicy Basil Tagliatelle

Roasted Scallops with an Apple & Fig Tart Finished
with an Orange & Lemon Sauce

A Scallop, Mussel, Crab & Ginger Ravioli with Sauted Oyster Mushrooms,
Served with a Light Mussel Nage

Pan-Fried Crab Cake Served with a Salad of Rocket and
Roasted Pine Kernels, Drizzled with a Light Herb Oil

Crab & Clam Risotto served with Mixed Leaves and Crispy Pieces of Parmesan

Caramelized Local Scallops with a Red & Yellow Pepper Compote
Enhanced by Herb Oil

Steamed Medley of Shellfish Served with White Coconut Cream Flavoured
with Lemon Grass, Lime & Ginger

wheelers menu 6

MAIN COURSES

Roasted Monkfish on an Olive and Sun-Dried Tomato Mash,
with Crispy Fennel Surrounded by a Coriander Pesto

Whole Dover Sole Layered with Asparagus and Glazed with Hollandaise Sauce,
Served with New Seasonal Vegetables

Poached Halibut Placed on a Fresh Pea and Pancetta Risotto,
Salad of Deep-fried Herbs and Horseradish Dressing

Fillet of Salmon Scented Lightly with Lemon and Cardamom, Rested on Sauté
New Potatoes, Griddled Asparagus and Remoulade Sauce

Roasted Cod Studded with Sweet Garlic and Pancetta
Served with Fresh Podded Peas and Lettuce, Accompanied by a
Caesar Dressing and Onion Rings

Baked Wing of Skate Served with a Spring Onion Mash,
Baked Vine Tomatoes and Salsa Verdi

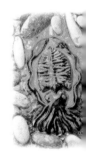

wheelers menu 7

STARTERS

A Risotto of Crab and Sweetcorn Finished with Rocket and
Scallops of Roasted Lobster

Freshly-Baked Lobster and Prawn Tartlet with a Herb Salad and
Drizzled Vinaigrette

Salmon Rillettes with a Lemon, Lime and Coriander Served
with Warm Speciality Bread of the Day

Pan-Fried Crab Cake with a Baby Spinach and Walnut Salad
Surrounded by a Herb Oil

Caramelized Scallops Served with Creamed Cabbage, Wild Mushrooms and
Bacon Served with a Light Chive Sauce

Pan-Fried Crab Cake with a Rocket & Watercress Salad

Roasted Scallops Rested on a Homemade Coleslaw
Finished with a Fennel & Leaf Salad

Squid Coated with Crispy Tempura Served with an Aromatic Cous Cous
Accompanied by a Sweet & Sour Sauce

wheelers menu 7

MAIN COURSES

Pan-Fried Cod on a Tartare of Crushed New Potatoes Accompanied
with Fresh Podded Peas, Wild Mushrooms, Glazed Onions Topped
with Crispy Parma Ham and Served with Sauce Verte

Roasted Monkfish Nicoise with Pommes Parmentier, Wilted Rocket
and Finished with Beetroot Crisps

A Mille-Feuille of Baked Skate and Basil Mash Topped
with a Soft Herb Crust Surrounded by a Ratatouille sauce

Caramelized Fillet of Sea Bass on a Dill and Citrus Pasta Accompanied with Glazed Baby
Vegetables, Pomme Dauphine and a Light Vegetable Nage

A Supreme of Cold Poached Salmon Rested on a Dill and Chive Potato Salad Served
with Local Kentish Asparagus, Celeriac and Drizzled with a Light Vinaigrette

Local Smoked Poached Haddock on a bed of Sliced New Potatoes, Leeks and a
Bacon Topped with a Poached Egg and Drizzled with a Light Mustard Sauce

Roasted Monkfish on a Cucumber Spaghetti Accompanied by Our
Own Local Cockles & a Fish Cream Sauce

Baked Skate, Buttered New Potatoes & Asparagus Served with Beurre Noisette

Seared Darne of Salmon with Shredded Mangetout,
Fritoe Potatoes & Sauce Mousseline

Grilled Lemon Sole Topped with a Ginger & Coriander Chutney,
Rested on a Tomato Fondue

One Whole Split Lobster with Salad

One Whole Cracked Crab with Salad

wheelers menu 8

STARTERS

Roasted Scallops Placed Around a Gateaux of Braised Lentils,
Creamed Mash potato. Served with Crispy Parma Ham
and Lemon Confit

Thinly Sliced Scottish Salmon Lightly Grilled. Served with a
Warm Salad of Lemon and Dill Gnocchi

Marinated Jumbo Prawns Skewered Roasted and Placed on a Bed of
Aromatic Cous Cous Drizzled with Sauce Vierge

Cannelloni of Prawns and Tarragon Set on Braised Fennel with Wilted Shavings
of Pecorino Enhanced by a Sweet Tomato Dressing

Pan-Fried Crab Cake Served with a Mache and Walnut Salad
Drizzled with a Light Herb Oil

Steamed Mussels in a Creamed Leek and Cider Sauce Finished with
Freshly Diced Tomato and Chopped Herbs

wheelers menu 8

MAIN COURSES

Pot-Roasted Halibut Gratinated with Citrus and Crab Hollandaise
Placed on a Sweet Potato and Coriander Mash

Seared Tuna on a Tian of Crushed Potatoes
Finished with Spring Onions and Herbs Accompanied with a
Warm Garnish Tossed in a Light Balsamic Vinaigrette

Baked Skate Wing Coated in a Grainy Mustard Crust
Set Upon Creamed Winter Vegetables.

A Rosette of Salmon Perfumed with Lime and Herbs Set on a
Red Onion Marmalade and Confied Winter Vegetables

Pan-Fried Cod with a Lemon and Herb Crust Garnished with a Gratin of Potato
and Leek Finished with a Sweet Red Onion Dressing

Local Smoked Haddock Set in its Own Creamy Mustard Broth
Served with a Poached Egg and Turmeric-Flavoured Potatoes
Finished with Tomato and Coriander

the oyster seekers

wheelers menu 9

STARTERS

A Trio of Salmon (confied, smoked and seared)
with a Golden Syrup and Caper dressing.

Roasted Scallops on a Bed of Minted Cous Cous
Served with a Coriander Tuille Biscuit
and a Blood Orange Dressing

Roasted Mackerel Cooked and Served in its Own Marinade
Scented by Coriander, Cardamom and Saffron

A Ravioli of Skate set on Caramelized Celeriac
with a Lemon, Caper and Nut-Brown Butter Dressing

Crispy Pieces of Marinated Squid Placed on an Olive, Roast Pepper,
Tomato and Basil Risotto.

Pan-Fried Crab Cake with a Rocket, Celery,
Apple and Walnut Salad

wheelers menu 9

MAIN COURSES

Seared Tuna with a Horseradish and Coriander Crust
Roasted on Herb-Glazed Mediterranean Vegetables Finished
with a Balsamic Dressing

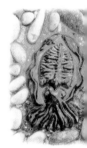

Roasted Fillet of Seabass with an Aubergine Caviar,
Baked Fennel, Chorizo Sausage and a Basil and
Parmesan Dauphine

Pan-Fried John Dory with Crushed Sweet Potatoes and a
Medley of Caramelized Salsify, Baby Onions and Pancetta
Served with a Sage Cream

A Risotto of Flaked Smoked Haddock
Finished with Spinach, Tomato and Grated Parmesan,
Topped with a Warm Poached Egg

Roasted Loin of Monkfish with Puy Lentils, a Rosti Potato
and Crisp Coppa Finished with Sauce Gribiche

Baked Cod on a Bed of Wilted Spinach Served with Lightly Curried
Mussels Finished with Fresh Coriander

the oyster seekers

wheelers menu 10

STARTERS

A Warm Salad of Buttered Artichoke and Poached Egg Laced
with Smoked Salmon and Glazed with Hollandaise Sauce

Caramelized Scallops with Wilted Rocket and Red Pepper Pasta
Dusted Lightly with Parmesan

Pan-Fried Crab Cake Served with a Salad of Tender Leaf Spinach
Finished with Toasted Pine Kernels and a Herb Oil

A Small Piece of Local Smoked Haddock Rested on a Light Macaroni Cheese
and Topped with Poached Quail's Egg

Jumbo Prawns Coated in a Light Sesame Seed Tempura Batter
Served with a Refreshing Marinated Cucumber Spaghetti

An Escabeche of Pink Bream Topped with a
Julienne of Deep-fried Celeriac

wheelers menu 10

MAIN COURSES

Cod baked with mustard and parsley crust, rested on a ham hock
and cabbage ragout, with buttered fondant potatoes and glazed baby carrots

Baked local skate wing, served with curried rope grown mussels,
spinach and red lentils

Roast fillet of seabass on braised sauerkraut with garlic dauphine potatoes,
roasted root vegetables and thyme sauce

Baked rainbow trout finished with grenobloise sauce
(capers, lemons, parsley and croutons) served with boulangere potatoes,
wild mushrooms and buttered spinach leaves

A casserole of seafood and shellfish poached in a saffron and garlic broth
with aioli sauce and buttered French beans

Grilled Dover sole with a cauliflower gratin, roast chateau potatoes
and caramelised salsify, garlic and broad bean ragout

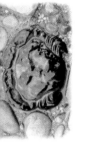

the oyster seekers

wheelers menu 11

STARTERS

Cushions of Potato and Lentil Soufflés,
Served with Roasted Scallops and Topped
with Fine Pieces of Crispy Parma Ham

Cod Brandarde Fritters, Served on a Bed of Pea Purée,
and Surrounded by a Traditional, Velvety Parsley Sauce

Baked Fillets of Red Mullet, Topped with Olive Tapenade
and Served with a Salad of Celery Remoulade and Garnished
with a Julienne of Deep-Fried Root Vegetables

Scottish Rope Grown Mussels, Steamed Open with
Wine and Vegetables, and Finished with Chopped Parsley,
Chervil and a Twist of Black Pepper

A Pan-Fried Crab Cake, Served with a Rocket and Walnut Salad
and Finished with a Light Herb Oil.

A Leek, Saffron and Potato Soup, Served with Local
Poached Oysters and Chive Chantilly

wheelers menu 11

MAIN COURSES

Pan-Fried Fillets of John Dory with a Goat's Cheese
and Basil Ratatouille, Accompanied by Roasted Asparagus
and White Bean Sauce

A Fillet of Cod Placed on a Ragout of Creamed Cabbage,
Wild Mushrooms and Bacon, Garnished with Steamed Mussels
and a Delicate Pea Veloute

Local Smoked Haddock, Topped with Welsh Rarebit and Rested on Champ,
Served with a Grainy Mustard and Chive Sauce

Pan-Fried Fillets of Sea Bass Placed on a Buttered Celeriac Fondant,
Surrounded by a Cassoulet of Haricot Blanc and Finished
with a Dice of Tomato, Parsley and Parma Ham

Caramelized Salmon with a Sesame Seed and Lemon Topping,
Served on Pommes Lyonnaise, and Garnished with Roasted Asparagus
and Piquillo Pepper Dressing

Griddled Tuna Placed on a Saffron, Chive and Chorizo Mash Potato,
Served with Crispy Fennel and a Tomato and Coriander Dressing

the oyster seekers

wheelers menu 12

STARTERS

Fresh Cannelloni Filled with White Crab Meat and Scallop
Served with a Refreshing Fennel and Cucumber Relish
and a Roast Lemon Dressing

A Fillet of Red Mullet Baked and Placed on a Saffron and
Chive Mash with a Roast Beetroot Dressing

A Delicate Spring Vegetable Soup Perfumed with Lemon Grass and
Finished with Basil and Lightly Poached Tiger Prawns

Pan-Fried Crab Cake with a Warm Potato and Watercress Salad

A Local Clam and Asparagus and Prawn Risotto Topped with
Fresh Parmesan Shavings

Pan-Fried Scallops with Puy Lentils and a Warm Vinaigrette of Baby Leeks
Finished with Gloustershire Old Spot Lardons

wheelers menu 12

MAIN COURSES

A Whole Lobster Poached in Aromatic Court Boullion
and Placed in a Feuillette of Puff Pastry served with Baby Vegetables
and Chive Beurre Blanc

Pan-Fried Guilt Head Bream Served with
Pomme Mousseline Fresh Podded Peas, Broad Beans,
Local Asparagus and a Horseradish Veloute

Roast Monkfish on a Warm Tartlet of Goat's Cheese
and Red Onion Marmalade Served with a Balsamic Caramel and
Rocket and Apple Salad

Roasted Seabass on Pesto New Potatoes with Barrigole Artichokes,
Rocket and Asparagus

Caramalized Local Skate on a Warm French Bean Mustard Caper
and New Potato Salad with Salsa Verdi

Pan-fried Cod on a Bed of Wilted Spinach Finished with Fresh Gruyère
and Allium Sauce Accompanied by Pomme Delmonaco

the oyster seekers

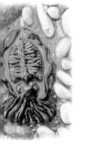

wheelers menu 13

STARTERS

A Seafood Paella

Roasted Scallops with a Warm salad of Wild Mushroom,
Black Pudding and Crispy Pancetta

King Prawns served with Baked Figs
Wrapped in Parma Ham, Stuffed with Gorgonzola and
Talegio with Balsamic Caramel and Rocket

Half a Lobster Served in a Filo Case with Tomato Confit, Asparagus,
New Potatoes and Mixed Pepper Dressing

Local Smoked Haddock Set in a Curried Leek and Potato Tart,
with a Warm Lentil and Mustard Dressing

wheelers menu 13

MAIN COURSES

Roasted Cod on Wilted Tender Spinach Leaves,
Surrounded by a French Onion Soup and Gruyère Twirls

Monkfish Scented with Lemon Grass, Accompanied by a Fondant Potato,
Courgette Tarte Fine and Olive Tapenade

Caramelised John Dory with Glazed Autumn Vegetables,
Roasted Garlic Mash, Parsnip Crisps and White Bean Sauce

Pan-fried Fillet of Snapper, Set Upon a Saffron, Chive and
Prawn Risotto Finished with Crispy Pieces of Squid

Fillet of Seabass with Creamed Leek and Fresh White Crab Accompanied
by Woodland Mushrooms, Parmentier Potatoes and Asparagus

Skate Wing Baked with Pesto Served with Griddled
Mediterranean Vegetable and Sauce Antiboise

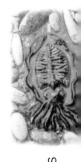

the oyster seekers

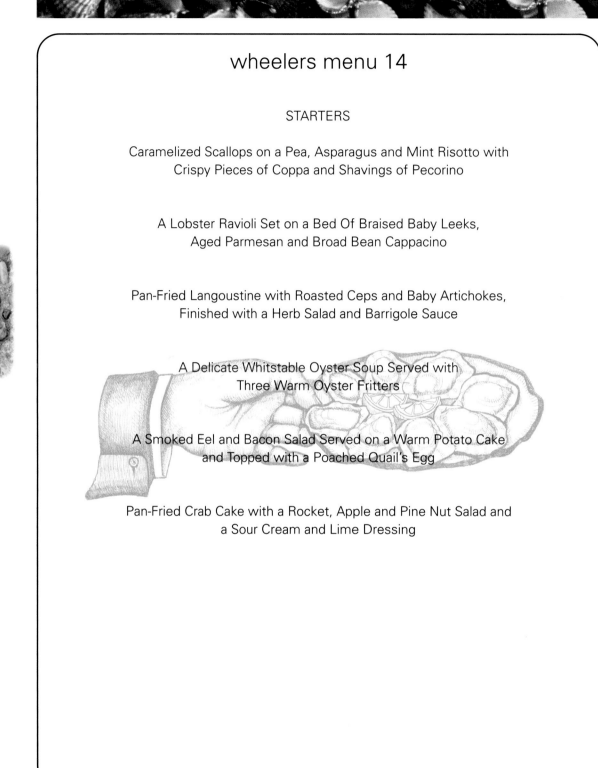

wheelers menu 14

STARTERS

Caramelized Scallops on a Pea, Asparagus and Mint Risotto with
Crispy Pieces of Coppa and Shavings of Pecorino

A Lobster Ravioli Set on a Bed Of Braised Baby Leeks,
Aged Parmesan and Broad Bean Cappacino

Pan-Fried Langoustine with Roasted Ceps and Baby Artichokes,
Finished with a Herb Salad and Barrigole Sauce

A Delicate Whitstable Oyster Soup Served with
Three Warm Oyster Fritters

A Smoked Eel and Bacon Salad Served on a Warm Potato Cake
and Topped with a Poached Quail's Egg

Pan-Fried Crab Cake with a Rocket, Apple and Pine Nut Salad and
a Sour Cream and Lime Dressing

the oyster seekers

wheelers menu 14

MAIN COURSES

Sesame-Roasted Tornadoes of Salmon wtih a Cauliflower
and Truffle Purée and Spring Vegetables

Rosemary-Scented Baked Cod with a Thyme
and Bacon Potato Cake, Fresh Podded Peas and a
Crisp Cannelloni of Ratatouille

Grilled Dover Sole Served with Parsley Buttered New Potatoes,
Tartare Sauce and Fresh Seasonal Vegetables

Baked Seabass on a Roasted Butternut Squash,
Red Onion, Thyme and Feta Cheese Tart Served with Crispy Pancetta,
Rosemary Sauce and Sweet Potato Crisps

Pan-Fried Skate Wing Coated in Beurre Noisette
accompanied by Salsa Verdi Croquettes and Steamed Vegetables
Stuffed with a Mint and Basil Ratatouille

A Savoury Caesar Salad Served with a Whole Warm
Whitstable Lobster and Finished with Classic Caesar Dressing,
Shavings of Aged Parmesan and Deep Fried Anchovies

the oyster seekers

recipes at a glance

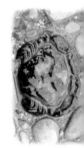

the oyster seekers

the oyster seekers

glossary

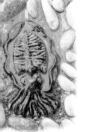

Banana Shallott	A long onion used in cooking, easy to peel and slice.
Clarified Butter	Butter that has had the water, milk solids and salt removed. This can be done by heating and then straining butter through muslin.
Devein	To remove the black vein that runs down the back of a prawn. It has a bitter flavour and should be removed before eating.
Lardon	A small chunk or strip of bacon or pork fat (smoked or unsmoked) to flavour dishes.
Mandolin	A sharp slicer used to slice julienne vegetables.
Papillotte	To cook food 'en papillotte' is to cook in paper or foil, in order to seal in flavour and use the steam generated to cook the food inside the parcel.
Shuck	To open the shell of an oyster with a small, thick-bladed knife.

the oyster seekers

picture credits

Jacket photographs and interior photographs of Whitstable and Wheelers reproduced by kind permission of Geoff Langan

Additional photographs on pages 19, 104, 106, 109, 115, 124, 135, 136, 160, 167, 168, 172, 174, 197 and 234 reproduced by kind permission of ENVY Design

Photograph of Whitstable sunset on page13 reproduced by kind permission of Brian Hadler

Food photography on pages 29, 32, 47, 49, 58, 69, 74-75, 84, 86, 89, 98, 107, 123, 129, 131, 139, 145, 149, 150, 155, 170, 182, 188, 201 and 203 reproduced by kind permission of The Anthony Blake Picture Library

Photographs on pages 86, 89 and 104 © Cephas Picture Library

Line drawings on pages xii, 36,78, 103,178, 187, 192 and 204 reproduced by kind permssion of Christian Furr

Fish preparation line drawings on pages 61, 81-83, 93, 119,142 and 195 reproduced by kind permission of Morgan Davies

Fish painting in photograph on page 120 © Siobhan Hewlett

copyright notices

bibliography

The Shell Book of Beachcombing by Tony Soper. David and Charles
(Newton Abbot, 1972)

The Wheelers Fish Cookery Book by Macdonald Hastings and Carole Walsh.
(Michael Joseph, 1974)

There's Time For A Meal by Ambrose Heath.
(Robert Hale, 1941)

History in Whitstable – Places and People by Geoffrey Pike and John Cann published by
Whitstable Improvement Trust, 1995

Oysters and Dredgermen by Geoffrey Pike, John Cann and Roger Lambert.
Compass Publications, Seasalter

Super Salads: Healthy Salads for Mind, Body and Soul by Michael van Straten.
(Mitchell Beazley)

English Recipes and Others from England, Scotland, Wales and Ireland,
As They Appeared in Eighteenth Century Cook Books by Sheila Hutchins.
(Methuen, 1969)

Madame Prunier's Fish Cookery Book, Revised. (Hurst and Blackett, 1959)

240

the oyster seekers

MANDY BRUCE 1954 – 2003

Mandy Bruce was the author of numerous biographies and children's books. She was also a highly successful Fleet Street journalist. Her great love was the seaside town of Whitstable, in Kent, where she and her husband Ross Tayne lived in a house on the beach. Mandy was a regular customer at Wheelers.

DELIA FITT opened her first oyster when she was ten years old – and she's been opening them in Wheelers ever since. She's lived with fishing – and the selling, cooking, catering and enjoyment of fish – all her life. She says she'll never leave Whitstable. 'I'd hate to live anywhere else. I love this hard north light – and the brown shrimps!'

MARK STUBBS took a job in the kitchens of Wheelers when he was just 15 – and decided there and then to become a chef. He trained in Thanet, where he won the Nestle Toque D'Or prize for the best student nationwide. He went on to train in France, at The London Intercontinental Hotel, under masterchef Peter Kromberg and then The Hyde Park hotel under chef David Nicholls. Now 27, he lives with his fiancée Nicola and, even off-duty, they can be found tucking into big platefuls of mixed seafood: 'Local lobsters. You can't beat them!'

GEOFF LANGAN is originally from Ireland and has worked as a photographer in the UK for twenty years. This is his second book for Blake Publishing. His first book, by sharp contrast, was twenty-four portraits of violent men. He is a passionate cook, and an amateur foodie. He lives near Bristol with his wife Rachel and son Patrick.

the oyster seekers

the oyster seekers

come and visit …

Wheelers
8 High Street
Whitstable
Kent
01227 273311

Whitstable Tourist Information
7 Oxford Street
Whitstable
Kent
01227 275482